"Darren Hibb o-
phetic visions a
clear road ma to
the impending upon America. His
book is both sobering and hopeful; convicting and
constructive. May God give us grace to heed its warning. Thank you Darren for your faithfulness to speak
the truth."

Pastor Scott McKay | Willow Drive Baptist Church
Lake Jackson, Texas

"This book takes readers down a path of vivid con-
templations with deep implications on both a national
and personal level. Hibbs asks the tough questions
and gives solid answers. Your understanding of God's
judgment will be shaped in new ways. Christians in
America and around the world need this message of
hope."

Pastor Steve Trevino | Cross Central Church
Bryan, Texas

THE YEAR OF THE LORD'S FAVOR?

A DRAMATIC VISION OF 9/11 TWO DAYS BEFORE IT HAPPENED AND HOW IT CAN CHANGE YOU TODAY

DARREN HIBBS

10WeekBooks.com

THE YEAR OF THE LORD'S FAVOR?

Copyright © 2013 Darren Hibbs
10 Week Books

Cover design by Steve Trevino

ISBN: 0988919516
ISBN-13: 978-0-9889195-1-8

10WeekBooks.com

This book is dedicated to my three beautiful children; you are truly gifts to your mother and I. I pray that this world and country you grow up in will be an even better place than it was for me. May God richly bless each of your cherished and beloved lives. And remember that no matter what, even if the fire comes, never bow to anyone but your Heavenly Father.

Contents

ACKNOWLEDGEMENTS

I want to thank my family for allowing me the opportunity to write this book. It is truly been a sacrifice for a young family that never stops moving and growing. Sarah, you have held up my arms more times than I can count, and I will be forever grateful.

Lord, you gave me this message and I pray I have stewarded it well. Thank you for Your voice, Your compassion, Your love, and Your gentle leadership. Give me grace to always offer You a seat at my table.

To my editors, Carolyn Nicholson, Keri Wurbs, Amy Brooks and Joanne Burnett, I thank you for the wonderful polish you have put on this book. I could not have done this without you.

To my in-laws, Ralph and Keri Wurbs; I never would have been able to write one word if it were not for your help, love and support. Thank you so much for all that you do.

To Steve Trevino, I want to thank you for your friendship and your remarkable eye for layout and design. You have made this book something I can be forever proud of.

Lastly, I would like to thank my parents, Doug and Diana Hibbs. You have always been supportive of everything I have tried to do. I would not be who I am today if it were not for your love, faithfulness and encouragement throughout my life. Thank you.

PREFACE

We live in tumultuous times. Repeated surveys and studies have shown that optimism that our future will be better than our past is way down. Are our best years behind us as a nation? As a planet?

I pray we have not crossed into a place where this is the case, but more and more it looks as though our resistance to God has caused us to slip further from a place of redemption. I choose never to give up hope that God can and will reach down into America and ransom the years that our locusts have stolen.

I pray you will not give up hope either. That is what this book is about. Never giving up hope. When we hear the prophetic words of the Lord, our future looks bleak, but we must remember that God's rebuke is never to punish us, but to bring us back to Him.

Pray with me that our best days are ahead of us. What will that take? Read on to find out.

FOREWORD

I have never been a fan of "Doomsday Prophets." Maybe that is because I have never been a fan of doomsdays, but I think it is really more than that. While it is difficult to hear about the judgment of God, it is almost as hard to endure the judgment of Christians. The latest earthquake, the latest hurricane, the latest terrorist attack—these are all the outcome, they proclaim, of some despicable human beings who need to repent or be left behind. America is headed to hell at a brokeback speed, so we might as well hunker down, buy guns, and vote red.

I feel torn because I do not identify even slightly with such sanctified judgment. On the other hand I do not relate to the tolerant church that heeds the values of a morally relative culture at the expense of God's timeless truth. Can't we find some middle ground between Bible-beating and Bible-ignoring?

Darren Hibbs strikes the balance America needs. I know Darren personally and have seen the way he interacts with "sinners." He loves them deeply because he considers himself one of them. Unlike many supposed prophets, Darren's message is not aimed at "those politicians" or "those homosexuals" or "those liberals." Rather, he issues a clarion call to the church: it is time for us—for US!—to repent.

I agree with Darren that God's judgment of nations is not just an Old Testament relic but a New Testament reality. In fact, one could easily argue that like any fireworks show, God saves the best for last. On the flip side I also concur with Darren that because God is predisposed toward mercy, there is hope for America. An epic Great Awakening is possible.

I have not had any revelations about God's plans for this infant empire, but Darren is someone I trust because of personal experiences with his prophetic intuition. I have encountered three major crises in my adult life, and I have known Darren while facing two of them. Although he lived in a different city at the time of their occurrence and had no way of knowing my situation, Darren prophesied to me exactly what I was going through, who it involved, and what God was doing in the midst of the chaos. His words sustained me like only words from God can.

I believe his words can do the same for the church in America.

Michael Rowntree
Senior Pastor | Wellspring Church
North Richland Hills, Texas

Chapter 1
SEPTEMBER 11, 2001

I had never had visions like these before. In fact, after these I was not sure if I had ever really had a vision before. What I thought were visions did not look like this. They were not this real and vivid.

These were gripping, eerie, and somewhat menacing. People were on fire, wrapped up like mummies or screaming out pleading for help. I could see their mouths through the bandages crying out or their faces in anguish, but I heard nothing.

Maybe that is what made them so chilling. I only saw the vision, but I did not hear them. The images are forever stained in my mind. I could not figure out what they meant. For two weeks I pondered why I was having these visions of people burning and in pain, and why was I having them on Saturday nights?

But I am getting ahead of myself.

KNOWING GOD HEARS

I grew up being taught that God does not speak anymore, but that all changed in 1995 when I met a prophet for the first time. I was not prophesied over, but the encounter started me questioning whether or not God did still speak. I decided that if He was still speaking, I wanted Him to speak to me, so I began asking.

I asked the Lord for over five years before I ever heard Him speak the first time. That first time was just a year before 9/11 when I had come back from a mission trip in Guatemala during the summer of 2000. It was a family friend, Loretta, who was going to be the one to prove to me that God really knew me and heard me.

One night in the mountains of northern Guatemala, I was sleeping on the floor of a pastor's house. His house was big; it had two rooms. The walls were made of hand-sawn lumber straight from the trees that had just been cut down. It ventilated well because there were up to two-inch gaps between the wall boards in places. The eves were open to the outside and there was no ceiling, but it kept most of the rain out. The roof was aluminum, so every drop of the torrential downpour we were in was magnified.

I was in a "mummy" backpacking sleeping bag trying to keep the gnats that seemed to be pouring into our bedroom from biting me. I had never met a gnat that bit before, but these guys seemed to like the way I tasted. I sealed myself inside the sleeping bag so that very little air was getting out and my breath was heating the inside to an uncomfortable temperature.

It was around 50 degrees outside, but I was sweltering inside my bag. I passed the time by trying to squish the gnats that were biting me. After what seemed like ten hours, I heard one of my companions I was sharing the dirt floor with stir.

"What time is it?" I asked.

"11:30," he responded.

"It's only been an hour since I went to bed!" I thought to myself.

I was in misery. I could not take this anymore. The gnats were terrible. It felt like thousands of them were biting me simultaneously at all times. I cried out to God:

"God, You've got to do something about these gnats! This is the worst night of my life!"

It was not the most spiritual of prayers, but it was definitely one of the most genuine in my life. About two minutes later one of my companions shouted, "I can't take it anymore!" and ran out of the room into the pastor's bedroom. We heard mumbling in the room next door and very shortly afterward Craig emerged with a coffee can filled with a smoking corn cob. We were all confused because the pastor did not speak Spanish and we did not speak his language.

"Craig, do you speak Ixil?" I asked him.

"Apparently," he smugly responded.

That was their solution. The only thing that hates the smoke of a burning corn cob more than people are biting gnats. The smoke was suffocating, but there were about two inches of fresh air right next to the dirt floor. That was enough. The gnats were gone and I was thrilled. I said a little prayer thanking the Lord and went right back to sleep.

A few weeks later I returned to Texas, and my parents and I sat down with Loretta. She started in with this story.

"I had a dream one night where you were being attacked by thousands of little demons and you were sweating profusely! The demons looked like little bugs. Your mother told me it was cold in the mountains where you were going but I saw you sweating. I heard you pray and ask for help."

I had not said a word to anyone about that story. Loretta could have only known that if God had shown her. She showed me the time she woke up and it just so happened to be 11:30pm, exactly when I had asked what time it was.

Six times Loretta read to me from her journal and each time she told me what happened on those six different occasions where I had cried out to God. He heard me each time, and spoke to someone else on my behalf in precise detail.

CHANGED FOREVER

That was a life-changing experience to know that God heard me, knew me, and saw me. He cared enough about me to speak to me prophetically through another person and tell me He heard everything I asked.

After Guatemala I was energized to seek the Lord even more to hear His voice. I was forever ruined to live without it once I knew He would actually speak to me. Over the next twelve months, He did not let me down.

One night I had a dream where I got a "0" on a test from a professor because he said I cheated. I woke up in a cold sweat because the end result of the dream was that I was kicked out of school because I got so mad at the accusation that I had cheated.

By the next morning when I went to that class, I had already forgotten about the dream. My professor came around at the beginning of class handing out tests, but when he slapped mine on the desk it had a big red "0" at the top.

I immediately looked at him and asked, "Why did you give me a zero?"

"Because you cheated," was his curt response; then he moved on to the next desk.

It was not until I was about to tell him what I thought of him that I remembered the dream. It took my breath away, literally. I could not speak when I thought about how God had warned me not to respond out of anger to something only He knew was about to happen within a few hours of my dream.

Over the course of a few weeks I was able to convince my professor that I had not cheated, but I was stunned that the Lord cared enough about me to keep me from getting angry at the professor. Instead, I was calm and won him over by gently asking him to reconsider, assuring him I had not cheated. In the end, he gave me a "100" on the test. I feel like it was God's way of showing me I had passed His test.

CLOSER TO HOME

Later that year I spent the summer of 2001 in Japan as a short-term missionary, and I had a wonderful time enjoying the beauty of Japan and the warm and hospitable people I met there. It was an enjoyable time of productive ministry where I built many beautiful relationships.

While there I had my third experience where God clearly spoke to me. I had a dream about my brother getting cut across his nose by a guy trying to stab him in the eye. In my dream he pulled his head back just in time and got a gash straight across his nose. People descended around him as the dream ended, and when I woke up, I cried out to God for an hour to spare my brother's life. When I got back to the U.S. a few weeks later, I went to visit him; he had a cut straight across his nose. He told me the story, and it was exactly like my dream. The Lord sent people quickly to protect him from his assailant since the blood from his nose blinded him.

I knew that the Lord involved me in what was going on with my brother, Richard, so I could partner with God in prayer. He wanted me to know what was happening and be part of the solution. God offered me the chance to partake in supernaturally saving my brother's life. God wanted my intercession at the moment of my brother's need.

When I pondered all this, it filled me with an unusual sense of excitement and anticipation. I was a senior in college now, so much of the anxiety that plagues a student was gone, and I was in a place where I was seeking God more and feeling His tangible presence more than I had ever felt before. That led me to start a new routine before going to bed.

I wanted to be more intentional about seeking God, especially in dreams, so I decided that I would incorporate a short little prayer into my bedtime routine.

"Lord, here I am. Speak to me."

It was just a short little prayer, but I wanted to go to bed with the Lord on my mind and willingly offer myself as a conduit for Him to speak. I knew I could not make God speak, but I was sure that the more I asked the more He would!

AUGUST 25, 2001

I did not do very well the first few weeks of trying out my bedtime routine. One of the hardest parts of asking God to speak is just remembering to do it. It does not take fancy words, just words. I probably only remembered to pray a few times that first week, but I did remember to pray on Saturday night.

I spent the evening of Saturday, August 25th, 2001, with some friends and had a great time. I came back to my apartment and spent some good time in prayer and reading God's Word. I went to bed with a feeling of God's great love over me, and I remembered to say my little bedtime prayer.

I got cozy under my covers, and just before I laid down I prayed, "Lord, here I am. Speak to me." Then I quickly laid my head down and closed my eyes.

I was not prepared for God taking my prayer so literally, so fast. That first vision started immediately. I saw people's faces streaming past me from right to left. As a person got closer to the center of my field of vision, they were magnified so I only saw their face. Each different person was in such great anguish from the flames that were in the background of my vision that their cries to me distorted their faces. These tortured souls cried out to me for help, but I heard nothing.

I was gripped for about 45 seconds to a minute before the vision ended as abruptly as it had begun. I was so shocked and perplexed by what I saw I sat up again. I have to admit that I was a little scared.

What did it mean? What was I supposed to do? I knew I was supposed to pray and ask God to show me the meaning, but I had no idea where to start. I was still so new to all this that I was confused as to how I was even supposed to begin. All the experiences I had hearing God up to now were so literal, and this seemed so mysterious.

I prayed for a while, but I eventually went back to bed after hearing nothing further from the Lord. One thing I was sure of was that I had heard from God. What I did not know was what I was supposed to do with it.

The next morning all I could think about was my vision. I pondered and prayed and pondered and prayed. At church I told the pastor, "I feel like people may feel like their world is burning. Maybe we can pray for them after the service." He agreed. He invited some people up afterward and we prayed for them.

I wish that instead of trying to interpret something I did not understand to make it fit my situation,

I had just told the pastor what had happened. I did not know back then that is what I should have done. It might not have changed anything, but I could have at least had help understanding it all.

SEPTEMBER 1, 2001

The next week I struggled again to make my new bedtime routine truly routine. A funny thing happened, though. That next Saturday night was almost exactly like the previous. I went to bed after having a great time with friends and after having a good bit of time in prayer and the Word that evening.

Remembering my experience from the previous week, I said my little prayer, laid my head down and closed my eyes. Immediately another vision appeared.

There was one person, wrapped up like a mummy, screaming from behind the bandages. Again there was fire behind him, and he was in utter torment. Was this hell? Was I seeing someone in trouble? My mind raced as the vision persisted. The person struggled to get loose from their mummy bandages but could not. Again, it lasted about 45 seconds to a minute and then ended as quickly as it had started.

I sat up in shock. This week I was really vexed. "What is going on?" I wondered. I prayed and prayed and pleaded with God to give me an answer. He spoke nothing, so I went back to bed.

The next morning I again pleaded with God for some clarity but I got nothing. Just like the previous Sunday, I told the pastor some strange line like, "I feel like people feel trapped. Maybe we should pray for them today." We had a prayer time at the end and prayed for people who felt trapped in their lives.

I look back on my attempts to understand a supernatural encounter without God's input as just silly. It makes me laugh and groan all at the same time.

SEPTEMBER 8, 2001

I made sure the following week that my Saturday evening routine stayed the same. I was not sure what to do with it, but I knew I had a formula for hearing from God so I was going to stick to it. I figured if I just kept hearing from God, eventually it would make sense.

That night I prayed my prayer, laid my head down on my pillow and closed my eyes with full anticipation of another vision starting immediately.

Nothing. I waited ten seconds and still no vision. Maybe God just needed a little more time.

I sat back up. I grinned as an idea flashed through my head. "I'll give God another chance," I thought. "It can't hurt!"

"Lord, here I am. Speak to me," I said. I quickly laid back down and closed my eyes. Again there was nothing. I waited for a minute with no vision and I finally gave up. I knew it was up to God to give a vision, but if He did not want to He did not have to. I knew I had not imagined them the two weeks before, and I was not going to force myself to conjure one up. I told the Lord "thank you" for the previous two weeks and quickly fell asleep.

But instead of a vision, I had a dream that night. In it, I was walking around lower Manhattan with an angel. I had never been to New York before and I had certainly never seen an angel, in real life or in a dream. In the dream I was excited to be in New York because I had always wanted to visit there. When I am excited about something new, I get very chatty. Apparently this is also true about me in dreams.

I went on and on as I told the angel what all the buildings were (I had studied them in college) and how excited I was to be there. It was as if he and I had been friends for a long time. I knew in the dream he was an angel, but I still treated him as a friend. I was not afraid of him so I used him as a sounding board. At one point I could have sworn I caught him rolling his eyes at me!

Other than his possible exasperation with me he was completely intense. He was unwaveringly focused on something, but I never stopped talking to ask what or why. He would not look at me or speak, he did not respond to anything I was saying and he led me around the city until we came to a particular place.

We abruptly stopped when we reached the place where he was leading me, and just as ominously as he had been walking, he stopped, turned and looked directly in front of him. I had not ever stopped chatting away about all the cool places I wanted to go see there until he stopped. His solemn face gazing into the distance finally put a stop to my relentless jabbering.

I had yet to turn and see what he was looking at. I looked into the angel's eyes as he gazed past me. He was so fixated on something, and it almost looked to cause him pain. I have never seen eyes like that since. They were not heavenly or otherworldly; they looked very human, but they were tortured by what was to come next.

SHEER TERROR

I finally turned and looked to see the World Trade Center's twin towers. I immediately lost my sense of sobriety of the moment and began chatting again about how I had always wanted to visit New York just to go to the observation deck of the World Trade Center. I jabbered away about how tall they were, how they were built and how much I admired them. The angel paid no attention to me whatsoever and again I closed my mouth as I realized my guide was in terrible pain over something.

Not long after I became quiet the angel held out his hand, open palmed, to point at the World Trade

Center. I looked down his arm past his hand toward the twin towers, and as soon as I laid my eyes on them they collapsed straight into the ground. I was puzzled why they had sunk straight down instead of falling over, but before I had too much time to ponder that, thousands of people started streaming past us.

Their faces were filled with horror, shock and terror. They came running at us quickly and before too long they were streaming past us by the thousands. Each one looked as if they were running for their lives.

As they streamed past us, I stood there unfazed and unaffected by what had just happened. I was so unaffected that I looked at my angelic guide and uttered words I have never stopped hearing ring through my ears since.

> "Well, that sucks! Now I'll never get to go up and visit the observation decks of those buildings!"

Again I could have sworn he rolled his eyes at me and that is when I got it. Finally I realized what had just taken place. My heart had been cold to the human tragedy that was taking place before me because I did not know how to put into context what was happening to me. As soon as I realized the World Trade Center had collapsed and there were possibly lots of people dead, I felt the grave reality that had so gripped the angel.

Shortly after I had gotten the point of what the angel was trying to show me, the dream changed. The buildings were gone, the people were back to normal and the place where they had been was leveled. The angel again held out his hand, open palmed, to point to what was coming.

I saw a small, white building grow up in the place of the twin towers. It looked about three to four stories high and on top I saw what looked like an amphitheater. People started gathering on top of the building and a band got on the small stage there. They began a worship concert and my heart was filled with tremendous hope.

There were 300 to 400 people on top of that building worshipping God, but the meeting ended quickly and I was disappointed. In the dream I knew that the people on top of that building were a small, holy group of people who had turned their hearts to worship God after the tragedy, but I was saddened that it was so short-lived and so small. Given the size of New York and the immensity of the tragedy, I expected so much more.

I immediately woke up feeling the sadness of the short-lived worship movement. I sat awake for quite some time pondering what had just happened. I had never seen an angel in a dream before and as of this writing I have not since. The whole dream was by far one of the most vivid and distinct things that has ever happened to me, awake or asleep.

I eventually went back to sleep, but when I woke up again it was all I could think about. I was asking God what it meant, and just like the previous two weeks I got nothing. I went to church that Sunday morning and, just like the last two weeks, told the pastor something I now think is so silly.

"I think this morning people feel like their world is falling down," I told him, trying to make something out of what I had experienced the night before. We prayed for several people and went to lunch. I could not possibly imagine God wanted to speak to me about something larger than my little sphere of influence.

I wish I had thought more about what the dream meant or that I had told someone to have them help me figure it out, but I did not. I did not think about the dream again. I left the church and it was not even a passing thought.

Well, not until...

SEPTEMBER 11, 2001

I woke up on Tuesday, September 11th, 2001 a little later than normal. I did not have anything pressing that day; I was a college student after all. My roommates had already gone to class, so I was enjoying a leisurely and quiet breakfast alone in my apartment. We had a 13" TV with rabbit ear antenna that we rarely watched; it sat unused as usual that morning. I ate my breakfast quietly, completely unaware the world had dramatically changed outside my door.

About 8:45 that morning my sister, Stephanie, called me.

"Darren, the World Trade Center just collapsed." Her tone was serious.

Waiting for the inevitable "gotcha" moment, I calmly replied, "Sure it did, sis. Sure it did."

"No, I'm serious. Planes flew into them and both buildings just collapsed."

We are practical jokers around our house, so I was not going to let her pull one over on me too easy, but I was not sure where this one could be going. I did not understand why she would be making a big deal out of this. Where was the joke?

I was not thinking at all about my dream. I have often wondered how the only dream I have ever had with an angel would not have immediately come to mind when she started in like this, but it just did not.

"Turn on the TV, Darren," Stephanie said. I could not remember ever hearing her voice shake like that before.

I turned on the little black and white television, but the picture was always slow to come on. It took a full 30 seconds for that old tube to warm up its pixels, but the timbre of the announcers' voices was all I needed to hear.

I do not remember how I ended the phone conversation with Stephanie. Those first thirty seconds of nothing but audio from my television seemed like an eternity. My dream came flooding back and replayed in my mind a hundred times before I saw my first glimpse of what had happened. Then, as we would all watch twenty times a day for weeks to come, I saw it.

The screen warmed up just in time for a replay of the first tower collapsing straight down into the ground. Then they replayed the second tower as it identically descended into the earth.

"Oh my God," I said as I dropped the phone to my side. "What have you done?" All I could think about was that I had already seen this. And just like that, a dream I had days before became my and everyone else in America's reality.

THE DAY THAT WOULD NOT END

Why had God shown this to me? What was going on here? What did this mean? A thousand questions raced through my mind as time stood still.

I was glued to the television for what seemed like the next ten years. Time stood still for so many Americans that day, but for me, all I could do was sit in silence as I watched the replay of my dream for all the world to see over and over and over again.

I cannot remember much else about that day except that I sat there watching the towers fall over and over again thinking about what I should have done. I thought time and again about how stupid I had been for three weeks. I kept thinking how silly I was to think God was showing me those visions and an angelic dream so we could have a cool Sunday service. All of a sudden I was overcome with guilt that I had not clued in.

"Maybe I could have stopped this," I told myself a hundred times that day. I kept asking myself, "Why did I not tell someone? Why would God have shown this to me if He did not want me to do something about it?"

I endured the rest of the day haunted by my thoughts. Haunted by what could have been. What should have been. I did not sleep that night. I could not tell my roommates what had happened to me. I could not tell anyone. I felt ashamed and embarrassed that I had been so foolish.

MAKING SENSE OF IT ALL

I lived in a fog for weeks after 9/11. I was so overcome by grief and guilt that I did not know how to cope. I spent most evenings alone after that trying to figure out why God had shown me those events three days earlier and why I had not done anything about it.

It came to a head as I found myself aimlessly driving around town one evening several weeks later. I quickly parked my car when I felt the surge of tears come over me. I laid my head into the steering wheel and cried out, "Why God? Why me? Why did you show this to me?"

"Because you're my friend, and I like to tell my friends what I'm thinking about."

As my head lay against the steering wheel, those words resounded through my body. Maybe I had not screwed up. Maybe I was not responsible for those peoples' lives after all. Maybe this whole thing was just God being a friend to me.

It seemed a little far-fetched at that moment, but those words brought instant comfort to my soul. I lifted my head up with a little more confidence. "If God knew these things were going to happen so that He showed me, He is smart enough to know that I was not going to do anything about it," I thought to myself. Maybe He really was just showing me what was on His heart.

I would like to say that I started feeling better about it all right then, but honestly it was months before I could let go of the idea that if I had said something, maybe I could have prevented thousands of people from dying. Honestly, looking back on it I am glad I did not. I am pretty sure now that if I had said something I would be prisoner #1 at Guantanamo Bay.

But nothing took away the question of "why?" Why me? Why that? Why an angel? Why the visions of people burning? God went to great lengths to highlight for me something that was going on in a place thousands of miles away.

As time went on, I could not help but think there must be something more that I was missing. Why would God go to such extraordinary lengths (at least from my perspective) to tell me about the most heinous act of aggression in America during my lifetime?

My answer came in another unexpected way.

Chapter 2
FREEDOM TOWER

A lot changed in my life over the next year and a half. Somehow, I was able to talk the girl of my dreams into marrying me. I had graduated college, started my first job and we were both leading a Bible study together in our little duplex. We took in a homeless girl hooked on drugs to help her get clean, and we were fasting as a couple. It was a crazy, fast-paced and joyous time in our lives.

Busying ourselves helps us put things behind us many times. It was probably my fast-paced lifestyle more than anything that helped me gradually cope with the guilt I felt over not stopping 9/11. I realize now that I was silly for having that guilt in the first place, but back then I did not know any better.

KEEP THE FIRE BURNING
Even with the confusion of my visions and dream about 9/11 and my busy life, I never stopped asking God to speak to me. And He was kind to keep answer-

ing. I had an encounter while visiting my friend David in Nashville where I cast many demons out of a guy. That was a new experience for me; it was exciting to know that God really did still entrust us with the same authority He gave to the disciples so long ago.

I was growing in my ability to ask the Lord to speak as I went about my day, and I was enjoying that. Marriage and work were exciting. We were forming some relationships in our Bible study that exist to this day. I am thankful for the incredible season of grace God gave us in those days.

All the while I had a secret hobby. America was bound and determined to rebuild from the ashes a new and improved World Trade Center. The country had a great preoccupation with what exactly was going to take the place of what our enemies had destroyed. I followed it all with great interest. I still was not sure what to make of my dream, but I was really paying attention to what was going on.

I am a construction guy so I like buildings. I kept up with the design process for the new building as soon as it became a topic of discussion. It was not long after the attacks that a sentiment began to grow that the towers should be rebuilt exactly like they were. "That would show 'em," was the thought process. Many "colorful" variations of new designs would mimic the old buildings. Most were not serious, of course, but were intended to be a gesture of our contempt for the enemies who would be so bold as to attack us at home.

It seemed like for some time every governmental leader with a microphone wanted to encourage New York to rebuild the towers as they were. Everyone was non-committal, of course, because a lot of money was at play, except to say that something would be rebuilt. The world would have to watch and wait to see what would come.

This is a broad generalization, but by early 2003 it seemed that most of the public sentiment on the matter was to rebuild two new towers much like they were before. Early proposals for the site were rejected in 2002, and the "drawing board" remained open. The Lord already knew what was on that board, though.

BACK TO NEW YORK

On March 15, 2003, I had my second dream about the World Trade Center. I was standing in Lower Manhattan at the base of the new World Trade Center building. As the dream started, I knew that is what I was looking up at, but I was confused because there was only one building. I had thought there were going to be two, and I was sure they would look something like the iconic twin towers. As I looked up at an unfinished building, it was already nothing like the towers that stood there before.

I was in a large, open plaza gazing up at a shiny and silvery-reflective glass-clad building. The glass exterior was about halfway up the building with the exposed steel rising up above that. The building was under construction and I was apparently there to work on it.

I went into the building and went up to near the top. I found about a dozen of my closest Christian friends helping with the construction. We were all there having a great time working on this new icon of American pride. There was a tremendous sense of "for God and country" with all of us working there. I remember several times how happy I was to get to be a part of this and smiling at my friends as we all enjoyed the history we knew we were making.

After working in several locations, I found myself on the top floor. The glass cladding was now up to about waist-high on the top floor, but the roof was not finished yet. I am not a big fan of heights, but I walked over to the half-wall to look over and see how high I was. I saw I was definitely at the top.

When I turned around, I noticed that all my friends but a few had left. Just then a faceless man walked into the room I was working in. The remaining friends I had quickly left me alone with this faceless man. I knew immediately the faceless man was Satan. A chill rushed over me as I tried to figure out what was going on. The sense of patriotism and honor quickly left, and now I was feeling confused and scared.

I kept my eyes on the ominous figure that stood about 15 yards away from me for fear that if I looked away he would try to throw me over the side of the building. To keep that from happening, I sat down against the half-wall of glass with my back to the outside of the building. I thought that if he was going to try to throw me over, at least I would see him coming and it would give me a fighting chance to escape.

As I sat there against that outer wall, the faceless man just stood and glared at me. We had a staring contest until finally he smiled and turned to walk away. I am not sure how I know he smiled since he was faceless, but that is how dreams sometimes are. His smile was almost giddy; it still gives me chills to this day. Immediately the dream changed, and the building was now done.

All my Christian friends and I who helped build the building were assembled on the top floor to take a tour of the building. The ominous feeling from when Satan was there was now gone, but the sense of patriotism and optimism had left as well. We toured the building from top to bottom taking the outer stairs to descend one floor at a time.

The dream was very bright and sunny from the beginning until now, but as we descended, each new floor became darker. Night was falling and the building became darkened. Each time we came to the stairwell now, we noticed it was leaking. Small drops of dirty water were dripping on us from the stairs above. With each new trip to the stairs, more water was leaking and each floor caused it to get dirtier. The leaks got so bad and the water was so dirty after a while all we were doing was trying to avoid getting dripped on.

The water became green and slimy; now there were what seemed like streams of water falling and it was impossible to keep it from getting on us. We were all so disgusted we agreed to cancel the rest of our tour and get out as quickly as possible. We all raced down the stairs until we came to the bottom floor where I pushed the exterior door open and walked outside to find myself alone on the dark plaza where the dream had started.

I was confused as to why I was alone as I looked up at the building. It was not a beautiful silvery-reflective building anymore but instead it was a dark, ominous tower looming above everything else. It had a sense of evil now and I felt horribly confused. I felt betrayed that the building so many of my Christian friends and I worked so hard to construct seemed to have been hijacked for evil. I thought to myself that this was not what I had signed up for.

After looking up at the building in great disappointment for some time, something caught my eye on the street below. I looked down and noticed a row of establishments all along the street. I did a double-take as all I saw were pornography shops and gay bars. I could not believe what I was seeing.

I sat there trying to figure it out. How had what so many Christians intended for good turned into something so wicked? I said out loud, "This can't be! It's not possible."

I was so dumbstruck by what I was experiencing that I had to go figure this out. I could not believe that these establishments were here at the base of this building that Christians had built. I walked down the street to see for myself; each new shop seemed more perverted than the last. I finally said, "I can't believe this. I have to see for myself." I felt angry and bewildered, so I walked inside one of the gay bars to convince myself I was not seeing what I thought I was. I walked in and was instantly grieved by what I saw inside.

One last time I said, "This can't be."

Immediately I woke up. As soon as I was awake, I heard the Lord's voice say, "That building will be a sign and seal of My judgment against America."

PUTTING IT TOGETHER

Those words shook me. The dream left me with a feeling of dread and those words haunted me. What was this going to mean? What was I supposed to do?

Since September 11, 2001, I had come to understand that I could not have done anything about the attacks. I still did not know why God showed me that, but I definitely knew this new dream was not about having a good Sunday service at church. Since all the talk was about rebuilding two towers, I thought the dream must have been figurative.

I immediately understood the meaning of several things in the dream. A sense of righteousness among God's people emerged to rebuild this tower (and America) and we would throw our support behind it. I knew that we (Christians) would lend our support to it, but that we should not have. I understood Satan was behind it the whole time, that at just the right time he would expose himself and the sense of patriotism would vanish.

I knew from the voice of the Lord I heard when I woke up that the completion of the building would signal a radical shift in our nation; God's patience for us would end. I also knew that homosexuality and perversion would have something to do with it as well, but I was not sure what. I figured only time would tell, so I "put the dream on the shelf" and went back to life.

OPENING MY EYES

Over the next several years the owners of the site began dragging their feet, irritating many leaders around the nation. It took quite a while to come to a final design decision, but when they did I was not surprised. A single building was chosen to replace the iconic towers. It was going to be a symbolic 1,776-feet tall and it had become colloquially named "Freedom Tower." Governor Pataki of New York gave it that name in a speech in 2003[1].

By 2006 the site construction was underway. I was again blown away by what I saw when they revealed the final design of the building. While I admit it is stunningly beautiful from an aesthetic perspective, I could not believe what I saw. The design renderings looked exactly like the building in my dream, especially the views of it at night. Freedom tower was to be a silvery-reflective glass-clad building looking nothing like the original twin towers.

My dream was turning out to be more than just symbolism. What I saw was taking place before my eyes. I began to watch very carefully as the months and years passed. The building remained a symbol of America's patriotism and freedom, and many warned that no one should dare tamper with the name, "Freedom Tower." And no one did.

Until 2009.

That is when the situation quickly began to change. The Port Authority of New York and New Jersey (the site owners) announced the new building would be named One World Trade Center, not Freedom tower. Changing the name of the tower seemed to knock the wind out of the sense of patriotism and honor the building stood for. Of course great outrage arose among a small minority of people, but it seemed like enough time had passed that most people did not really care.

9/11 MEMORIAL DEDICATION

Then came September 11, 2011, the day the 9/11 Memorial opened at Ground Zero. I watched on my television as they showed all the families waiting in anticipation to enter the site and find their loved ones' names etched into the stone facade. The camera crew took a shot looking up at the new tower, 1 WTC, from the open plaza. At that moment I realized the scene I was seeing was exactly what I saw when my dream began. The building was incomplete with steelwork going on at top but the silvery glass-cladding was about halfway-up the unfinished building.

I watched in amazement as if the Lord had shown me in 2003 the very scene I had seen on television in 2011. This forced me to contemplate the true meaning of the two dreams and how they were related. I began to ask the Lord what this all meant to the future of our nation. What were we to do?

I began thinking about how the past ten years had seen such unbelievable change in our nation, especially in regard to the church's increasing complicity with darkness. It seemed every new evil our culture and government introduced, the church was behind it 100% in the name of "for God and country."

HOW THEN SHALL WE LIVE?

What I have seen and concluded over the past twelve years is what I have to share in this book. We have been offered a great opportunity as a nation, but our time is running out. This historic and iconic building will be completed very soon. Whereas I do not believe that the great evil of our nation is a building, I do believe the Lord spoke to me very clearly that the building would be a literal sign of His coming judgment, a timing marker of things to come.

But I believe we still have hope. I choose to never give up on the grace and goodness of God. In every proclamation of judgment in the Bible there is always a call to repentance. He is always lovingly pleading for change, but not as an angry God seeking to destroy.

I want to clearly lay out what I believe is our hope for America while also clearly stating what the consequences of a failure to do so are. I believe our best hour may still be ahead of us, but it will require great change on the part of God's people, change I have not yet seen in earnest.

[1] Amy Westfeldt, Huffington Post, March 28, 2009. http://www.huffingtonpost.com/2009/03/28/critics-call-freedom-towe_n_180350.html

Chapter 3
HOPE AND CHANGE

Barack Obama was elected with a most unusual campaign slogan. Politicians running against an opposing party often run on platforms espousing change from the status quo, but President Obama's change was very undefined. It was as if the nation was so ready for any change at all that just the word inspired people.

Enough people in America recognized that we were heading down the wrong path that this vague idea of "hope and change" motivated them not only to elect Barack Obama but also to give him a Nobel Peace prize just for proposing such a notion. By giving him a Nobel Peace prize not for anything he had done, but simply suggesting that he would be different, the Nobel Committee showed just how bad the sentiment was about our current state.

One group was very vocal against President Obama and has remained so ever since: conservative Christians. The demographic group that was credited with electing George W. Bush was left out in the cold on January 21, 2009. The dramatic shift in political discourse and sensibilities since inauguration day, especially in regard to America's treatment of the conservative Christian voting bloc, has intrigued me. The nation has clearly seen our troubles and has completely rejected these conservative Christians and their ways.

Politically speaking, I cannot blame anyone for that. For over ten years now we have committed thousands of lives and untold financial resources to fighting an enemy we cannot see and one we are not sure if we are defeating or strengthening. It is disheartening to continue to fight a war where we cannot declare a victor. As almost all Americans, I am troubled by the partisan divide that has erupted on both sides of the political discourse in recent years.

I am troubled even more by what I have seen in regards to the two dreams the Lord gave me. Before I delve into any implications, let me first take a moment to discuss the landscape of America I believe the Lord was showing me in the two dreams.

WHY THE TWO DREAMS?

I have often wondered why God spoke to me so clearly through my two dreams in regard to what has become known as Ground Zero in New York. For years I struggled with a deeper meaning the Lord was speaking to me. I do not claim to fully understand everything the Lord is saying now, but I have a much clearer picture than I ever have before.

First, New York has and always will be a symbolic heart to America. Washington DC may be our current capital, but New York was America's first national capital and it still serves as our cultural and financial capital today. The terrorists who knocked down the twin towers knew they were not knocking two random buildings down, but they were targeting the heart of our nation's financial strength, Wall Street.

Even those of us who did not live in New York were touched deeply by the events of 9/11. Even though the stock market has had a couple of recoveries since the plummet following that day, there has been an ever-eroding confidence in the public's eye in our financial system. Pensions, 401K's and other investments have suffered since that day like no one would have imagined. No matter how much a Southerner or a resident of the Western United States may want to believe they are disconnected from anything that happens in New York, the truth is New York holds many of the keys to our nation.

New Yorkers know this; they often have quite a big head on their shoulders because of it. I am from Texas and many people here may not think so, but the fact remains that New York City is more than just a symbolic figurehead for our nation; what happens there affects us all.

God was not just showing me two dreams about New York City but about our nation as a whole. I believe He was using these two dreams about two very important watershed events in our nation's life.

I knew at the time I had the second dream about the forthcoming "Freedom Tower" that the two dreams were related, but I was not sure how. I was even more confused as to why God sent an angel as a guide to me in the first dream. If I had just seen the buildings collapse and the people rush in terror at me, it would have been enough to convince me I had received a dream from God without an angel. So, why the angel?

WHY THE ANGEL?

First, God still uses angels just as He did in the Bible. They are still His messengers when He has important messages to relay. When we have encounters with angels they cause us to really pay attention to what is going on. Every time God used angels in the Bible they put an exclamation mark on what was being said. He did not use angels every time He gave a message. Often a prophet was all He used, but when He did send an angel with a message it was always important.

Angels can be used to bring important personal messages, but more often God releases them to give important corporate messages. God telling me two days before our generation's greatest tragedy what would happen was not just a message for me or my church's Sunday morning service; it was for America.

The angel God sent has caused me to take this message very seriously, and it is why I write this book today. I believe that the first dream God gave me about the towers falling down was not the message, but an alarm. That is why God sent the angel, to alarm me that something very big was going on. The message God had for America was in my second dream.

IS THERE HOPE?

That message is not a comforting one. It has left me many times wondering, "Is there still hope for America?"

The answer is a definite "maybe."

Maybe, because what happens from here depends on God's people and how we respond. I will tell you plainly that I do not believe we have responded very well so far.

The hope that this nation is crying out for has not been given to them by the "conservative Christian" right thus far. The depth of distrust America has with the "Christian" right today is exemplified in the fact that Barack Obama easily won re-election. No incumbent president in his situation in the past has ever had a prayer of being re-elected. Unemployment, deficits, debt, international conflicts and low approval ratings have always spelled political doom for candidates in his position in the past. So why did America re-elect him? Because they do not believe "conservative Christians" have the answer.

Most Christians have blindly followed political talking points into bailouts for greedy bankers, wars, increasingly giving up our rights to the state and of most concern to me, using their political power to self-righteously and aggressively push an agenda and standard they themselves could not live up to. Christians have been co-opted by politics in this nation. In the nation's eyes we no longer stand as a people set apart for the will of God, but as one with a political party.

WE HAVE ONE TRUE HOPE

When our nation turned to a message of "hope" that was not offered by the only true Hope this world has, it should have caused we Christians to seriously pause for reflection. I have not seen that reflection but I pray I do soon. Politicians will never offer the hope that our nation needs, and the longer Christians look to them to supply hope, the more hopeless our nation will become.

I am not trying to demonize Barack Obama with this book. I hold him in great respect. I think his election was very historic in that a nation founded with the blight of slavery codified into our constitution would choose a black president.

So many great things have embodied his election and presidency so far, but the godless agenda that has advanced in our nation in the past several years is a symptom of a disease that lurks just under the surface. It is not a disease owned by one party or another; it is equally shared by all Americans.

Specifically, abortion and homosexual marriage rights are two very critical issues we have seen rapidly progress in recent years. Instead of open discussions about these issues, we have seen the public discourse degrade into an attitude of "if you are against these things then you are a neanderthal." That is very troubling to me and it means that Christian values no longer hold any prominent place in the public discussion. Since Barack Obama's re-election, many Republicans have shown their true colors by choosing to abandon the pro-life and pro-marriage agendas in favor of platforms they believe will keep themselves in office.

If ever there was an event that should awaken God's sleeping people, it is this: that so many politicians we believed to deeply hold our values have abandoned them in favor of public support.

So, is there hope?

Maybe.

Maybe God's people will stop relying on politicians to change things. Maybe God's people will stop relying on their 401K's for sustenance. Maybe God's people will cry out to our One True Hope in repentance and humility for true hope and change.

GOOD NEWS OR BAD NEWS FIRST?

The message from my dreams was clearly a warning. There is a day of judgment proclaimed against our nation that will not be turned back if we do not turn before then. But we can still turn it back! We should not despair, but we must act quickly.

When we are told there is bad news and good news and we are given a choice of what we want to hear first, most of us choose the bad news first. The good news is what I want you to take away from this book, so do not quit reading before you get to it.

Chapter 4
THE BAD NEWS FIRST

The term "judgment" is often misunderstood by people in context to God. For many reasons good and bad people have equated judgment as a horribly negative idea when God is involved. A great distrust towards Christians rises when we use that most loathsome "j" word.

People have no trouble understanding judgment properly when it comes to our court system. There, we know that judgment has to do with separating the innocent from the guilty. Americans know what "good judgment" means when speaking of someone who routinely makes sound decisions. But for some reason we have added an unnecessary connotation to judgment when it pertains to God.

Our judges all over the country judge and we accept that. People make business judgments all the time, and we accept that. Parents make character judgments about the people their children should and should not associate with every day and it seems normal. Why is God the only one in America that is unjust when He judges?

In Revelation 19:1-2 we find out that all heaven very clearly proclaims God's judgments to be righteous.

> 1 After this I heard what sounded like the roar of a great multitude in heaven shouting:
>
> "Hallelujah! Salvation and glory and power belong to our God,
>
> 2 for true and just are his judgments. He has condemned the great prostitute who corrupted the earth by her adulteries. He has avenged on her the blood of his servants."
>
> Revelation 19:1-2

Here we see God sitting as judge over the evil harlot Babylon who led the whole world astray in the last days. God has destroyed the ones who persecuted and killed His people throughout Revelation, and everyone agrees that He is just in doing so. God's judgment is not an arbitrary punishment of someone who never saw it coming. No, God's judgment is just like we understand from our court system here on earth, but a much more perfect version of it.

Something drastic has happened in America where people no longer trust God to be a just judge. There is a sentiment that He is not a divider of right and wrong but an angry assassin waiting for an opportunity to destroy us all. This is of course a lie straight from our adversary, Satan, but we as Christians must see that we have some responsibility for this too.

QUOTING GOD'S JUDGMENT

The biblical judgment that seems to come to people's minds most often today is of Sodom and Gomorrah, especially since it had to do with homosexuality. Many people have used it as an example of God's wrath and judgment against a nation that would endorse homosexual marriage. I have heard many politicians and public figures quickly reference it in an interview and then when questioned in detail on their thoughts they reply, "Well, I've never actually read the story before."

People have become increasingly distrusting of Christians for using biblical stories, mostly inappropriately, to justify their own prejudices. Outsiders are often correct in their assertion that Christians are filled with hate and justify their position with scripture. There are many shining examples where that is not the case, but I have seen far too often that Christians point to the few good examples to the exclusion of the myriad of bad ones.

The sad truth is that the story of Sodom and Gomorrah is a perfect example of God's *righteous* judgment against mankind and most people who refer to it have never even read it with understanding.

The story starts in Genesis 18 when God sends two angels to meet with Abraham.

> 20 Then the Lord said, "The outcry against Sodom and Gomorrah is so great and their sin so grievous 21 that I will go down and see if what they have done is as bad as the outcry that has reached me. If not, I will know."

Genesis 18:20-21

What is important to see here is that God says there is an "outcry" against Sodom and Gomorrah. Where is this outcry from? Who is making it? These are the keys we must focus on to rightly understand God's judgment.

We have many examples in scripture of an "outcry" reaching God. When the Israelites were oppressed in Egypt, God said He could not turn away from their cries any longer. Each time the Israelites cried out to Him from their oppression in the book of Judges, He heard them and saved them. God hears every cry of injustice. He listens to every call for justice. Many times He is patient with people, offering them opportunities to repent before He sits on His throne to dole out judgment between two parties.

So we see here that God was not arbitrarily punishing Sodom and Gomorrah, but that God is doing what any judge does--adjudicating between two parties. One party is those offended and oppressed by

Sodom and Gomorrah's wickedness and the other is the evil inhabitants themselves.

One confusing aspect of this story is that God seems to need two angelic witnesses to visit the city to confirm what He has heard. Should not God already know? Does not God know everything? Of course He does, but God is so concerned with His judgments being righteous He goes the extra step to put two eye-witnesses on the ground to give their report.

God is the one who gave the law that said, "On the testimony of two or three witnesses a man shall be put to death, but no one shall be put to death on the testimony of only one witness." (Deuteronomy 17:6) Even though the witness of God and those who cried out to Him were enough, He sent an extra two witnesses to record this for our sake. God is kind enough to us to go out of His way to prove to us that His judgments are just, true and righteous.

HOMOSEXUALITY

That brings us to the question of homosexuality. Most conservative Christians say the sin Sodom was judged for was homosexuality. Let me be very clear. Sodom's most grievous sin was not homosexuality.

America's problem is not homosexuality.

Many conservative Christians wield the story of Sodom and Gomorrah to show why God hates homosexuality. They would be wrong, while most liberal Christians and non-Christians who want to wield the Bible to defend indefensible practices say that Sodom was not judged for their homosexuality but for other sins. They would in fact be mostly right, but not for the reason they think.

What we see in Sodom is that the level of depravity had grown so bad that the men there were willing to kill in order to rape two angels, whether they knew they were angels or not. They would not even accept Lot's daughters he so "hospitably" offered to them in exchange for his guests. Their lust raged within them for illicit homosexual encounters so nothing would have stopped them short of the angels who blinded all of them.

It is obvious then that homosexuality truly was one of the sins that had taken hold of Sodom and Gomorrah, but homosexuality was not the reason for Sodom's judgment. For a better understanding of why that is, we need to turn to Romans 1 and see what Paul has to say about it.

When men and women suppress the knowledge of God, they have no other place to turn but to sin. Paul tells us in Romans 1:20 that all men can clearly see the existence of God from nature itself but that we choose to rebel against Him. We have no excuse for not worshipping Him, so God gives us over to the sin we desire out of our rebellion. When God gives us over to that sin, a snowball effect begins to happen.

24 Therefore God gave them over in the sinful desires of their hearts to sexual impurity for the degrading of their bodies with one another. 25 They exchanged the truth of God for a lie, and worshiped and served created things rather than the Creator–who is forever praised. Amen.

26 Because of this, God gave them over to shameful lusts. Even their women exchanged natural relations for unnatural ones. 27 In the same way the men also abandoned natural relations with women and were inflamed with lust for one another. Men committed indecent acts with other men, and received in themselves the due penalty for their perversion.

Romans 1:24-27

Here we find here that homosexuality is not the sin God judged Sodom and Gomorrah for, but the symptom of the true problem that led them to judgment. Paul makes it clear that homosexuality is unnatural. We can clearly see that from nature. Procreation, the act that keeps all life on earth continuing, requires male and female. Homosexuality goes against that natural order of life producing life. Homosexuality can only produce death, as all sin does. But what Paul says here is that society accepting homosexuality is the result of the evil already at work in those people.

Accepted by a society, homosexuality is the sign of depravity, not the reason for it.

THE TRUTH OF GOD

Killing babies in the womb is certainly depraved, but we do not immediately go from serving God to murdering innocent children. These are only signs that we have replaced the truth of God for a lie. God is letting our own depravity play itself out.

In Romans 1, Paul is speaking of a group of people who have chosen to turn what is right and wrong upside-down. When we see homosexuality embraced as an acceptable lifestyle, that means the other sins Paul speaks of in Romans 1 have already happened. When men and women view an unnatural behavior as acceptable, that means their moral compass has already been destroyed. Those people have already become morally bankrupt.

Sodom and Gomorrah were not judged because they were gay. They were judged because every manner of evil was permitted there. Homosexuality was just the God-ordained outcome of a people who exchanged the natural revelation of God for a lie. Paul concludes Romans 1 with this statement:

> 32 Although they know God's righteous decree that those who do such things deserve death, they not only continue to do these

very things but also approve of those who
practice them.

Romans 1:32

Clearly, societal acceptance of homosexuality is a
sign of impending judgment, not the only reason for
it.

RAPID ADVANCE

Much of the church has gotten it wrong here for
generations. There has never been a day or a place
where some people have not struggled with and given
into homosexual lifestyles. Just like any other sin, it
has existed for all generations. What has been different in our generation is that we have seen a rapid advance in it as well as a lighting-quick acceptance of it
in the last several years.

In May of 2012, President Barack Obama became
the first president to endorse homosexual marriage.
Almost immediately the national dialogue switched
from homosexual marriage being a sticky subject to
one that deserved universal acceptance. Quickly a
witch-hunt ensued to find every last bastion of hold-
outs for the neanderthal position that gay marriage
was wrong. Chick-fil-A bore the brunt of a full assault
on anyone who stood for a traditional definition of
marriage.

Dan Cathy, the president of Chick-fil-A was
quoted by a Baptist news outlet as supporting tradi-

tional marriage. Dan Cathy said nothing disrespectful of gay people, only that he and his leadership team personally held the position that only heterosexuals should be allowed to marry. This set off a firestorm where Chick-fil-A was branded as a league of hate-mongers.

The moral fabric of the nation seemed to have been turned upside-down overnight. Those who tried to do good were labeled as haters. Those who advocated for a license to sin were lauded as champions of justice. But this did not happen overnight. And it did not happen without the direct input of the church.

Again, Chick-fil-A may indeed be a good example of truth with humility, but to deny the overwhelming chorus of bad eggs out there would be foolish. Many have abused, teased, hated and made bigoted decisions based upon people's sinful struggles.

MAKING IT WORSE

All we need is to look back at church history to understand what has been happening in America. Throughout history, God's people have often been oppressed, persecuted or lacked any voice in politics. But when God's people draw near to Him and cry out for help, freedom and righteousness in their community, God answers. There are too many examples to list, but when God's people seek Him earnestly and commit to living righteously before Him themselves, nations are changed.

Europe became a "Christian" continent because a relatively small and oppressed minority of people cried out to their God who gave them such supernatural power that the pagans around them became jealous. These Christians had a God who loved. They had a God who cared. They had a God who healed, saved, delivered and provided. No god of this world they had known could do what the One True God could. It was not political power that changed nations, but the humble cry of simple believers following their Savior.

It is normal for God's people to change nations. It is actually our mandate that we go into "all the earth" and make disciples. As disciples multiply there comes a critical mass that forces societal change. It is our destiny to bring about societal change as thousands and even millions come to know their Creator.

So what does that tell us when seemingly thousands of Americans cry out every Sunday for a nation that continues to recede into the dark recesses of abominable sinfulness and shame? Why has the world's great "Christian" nation not been able to stop abortion? Homosexuality? Theft? (we have led the way with Internet piracy) Pornography? (again, we lead the way). Why does it seem like America is an inventor of new ways to sin?

Why are God's people seemingly powerless to affect change in our culture? It seems the more we try the worse we make it. How can that be?

Think for a moment of all the men in recent years who have been discovered to have secret sin exposed in their lives to the destruction of their reputation and careers. Pastors exposed as secret homosexuals. Politicians who have lobbied for stricter moral legislation caught with prostitutes or in lurid relationships. Were you to start a tally, the list would grow quickly.

WHAT WENT WRONG?

That is when the cold hard facts are cruel to consider. The divorce rate in America is nearly identical inside and outside the church[1]. The abortion rate is about thirty-five percent; again, nearly the same inside and outside the church[2]. Many pastors admit to willfully viewing pornography[3], let alone those people who simply attend their churches. Most pastors also admit that they spend between 1 hour and 6 hours in prayer per week: that is between just 8 and 51 minutes a day[4].

What happened is that we, as God's covenant people, have traded in our high position as overcomers of this world to instead dip our toes in the dangerous waters of secret sin. If God were to judge those being oppressed, murdered, persecuted and silenced right now, He could not differentiate between the church and the world because we are in the camp of the accused as well.

In fact, when God judges He will judge the church first because of His love for us. God's plan is that none should be lost but that through His people the redemption of the world would be brought in by the knowledge of His son. We as God's people are too bound up in sin to be effective.

What is worse is that when we as God's people hold political power, God expects much more of us.

> 10 If you falter in times of trouble,
>
> how small is your strength!
>
> 11 Rescue those being led away to death;
>
> hold back those staggering toward slaughter.
>
> 12 If you say, "But we knew nothing about this,"
>
> does not he who weighs the heart perceive it?
>
> Does not he who guards your life know it?
>
> Will he not repay each person according to what he has done?

Proverbs 24:10-12

And He also says:

> But the one who does not know and does things deserving punishment will be beaten with few blows. From everyone who has

been given much, much will be demanded;
and from the one who has been entrusted
with much, much more will be asked.

Luke 12:48

In America, Christians have been given much. Our forefathers handed us a "Christian" nation. The legal code and moral fabric is directly descended from Christianity, and Christians have almost entirely held legislative power for the entire history of our nation. I cannot imagine God expecting more from many nations in history.

God also requires that we stand up for the oppressed. We must stand up for those being slaughtered; those whose innocent voices are continually silenced. Every week sexual immorality is taking place in almost every church in America. It is a challenging thing to address, but it largely goes silently avoided, leading to secret pain, shame, abortion and family destruction. The church has given little time, attention and money to rescuing those innocent lives perishing at the hands of injustice.

GOD'S DISCIPLINE

Paul tells us something particularly incriminating of us today:

1 Does any one of you, when he has a case
against his neighbor, dare to go to law before
the unrighteous and not before the saints? 2

> Or do you not know that the saints will
> judge the world? If the world is judged by
> you, are you not competent to constitute the
> smallest law courts? 3 Do you not know that
> we will judge angels? How much more mat-
> ters of this life? 4 So if you have law courts
> dealing with matters of this life, do you ap-
> point them as judges who are of no account
> in the church? 5 I say this to your shame. Is it
> so, that there is not among you one wise man
> who will be able to decide between his breth-
> ren, 6 but brother goes to law with brother,
> and that before unbelievers?
>
> 7 Actually, then, it is already a defeat for you,
> that you have lawsuits with one another.
> Why not rather be wronged? Why not rather
> be defrauded? 8 On the contrary, you your-
> selves wrong and defraud. You do this even
> to your brethren.

1 Corinthians 6:1-8

God has given us the high privilege of not only judging the world but also the angels. That may seem far-fetched but when Jesus returns to judge the world He told us He would grant to those who overcome the right to "rule the nations" with Him (Revelation 2:26-27).

How can God give us the right to judge if we bear the same sinfulness as the world around us? Will not God purge our sin from us to make us clean and white like He promised? (Revelation 3:5) Certainly He will!

We must understand that if God is going to judge our nation for the sin and lawlessness that exists here, He will certainly start by disciplining a church which has held considerable authority over its culture and direction. If our nation deserves judgment, then the church as a whole doubly deserves correction.

It is important to understand that God will judge the church the same as the rest of the nation when He judges America. His purpose for the believers and the unbelievers is that both would repent and turn to Him.

As His people, we have a profound responsibility to proclaim this truthfully.

[1]Audrey Barrick (citing Barna Group statistics), Christian Post, April 4, 2008.
http://www.christianpost.com/news/study-christian-divorce-rate-identical-to-national-average-31815/

[2]Guttmacher Institute.
http://guttmacher.org/media/presskits/2005/06/28/abortionoverview.html

[3]The Leadership Survey on Pastors and Internet Pornography, Christianity Today, Winter 2001.
http://www.christianitytoday.com/le/2001/winter/12.89.html

[4]Audrey Barrick, Christian Post, December 28, 2009.
http://www.christianpost.com/news/most-senior-pastors-work-at-least-50-hour-weeks-42453/

Chapter 5
TRUE AND RIGHTEOUS

As God's people, we are required to understand that His judgments are always righteous. The unbelieving world always struggles to see God's judgments as righteous. They have little hope of accepting God's correction if His holy people do not acknowledge that everything He does is good.

We see in Revelation 16:5 that after a particularly harsh judgment against the world, even the angel who carried it out seems a little taken aback. He reaffirms that God is just in judging the world as He has and all heaven agrees with him:

> 5Then I heard the angel in charge of the waters say:

> "You are just in these judgments, O Holy One, you who are and who were; 6 for they have shed the blood of your holy people and your prophets, and you have given them blood to drink as they deserve."

> 7 And I heard the altar respond:

> "Yes, Lord God Almighty, true and just are your judgments."

Revelation 16:5-7

If God chooses to judge America, it will be because He has good reason. The cries of the oppressed and downtrodden will have reached His ears and overcome Him to the point of action. When He does this, He will be totally just in doing so. If God does not relent from judgment, then we as His people must stand in agreement that our nation, and we His church, deserve it. We must stand up and say that God is just in His judgments even if we bear the pain of them as well.

This is no small struggle for people whether they follow God or not. It has always been a struggle. The Psalmists reiterated this over and over again when he declared, "The Lord is good and His mercy endures forever," (Psalm 100, 107, 118, 136 and many more). David even instructed the singers in the tabernacle and temple to sing about this often (1 Chronicles 16:34).

WHAT DOES GOD JUDGE?

I have said that the church deserves judgment the same as our nation, but I have not yet clearly defined why God will judge. God is very clear on this, and it is worth careful investigation.

As I said before, it is not because of homosexuality. Homosexuality is a sign, much like the building in my dream, that the reasons for God's judgment have manifested themselves.

So let me clearly lay out why God judges and what He judges when it comes to nations, rulers and peoples. His judgments are different for society than they are for individuals. We must understand that as individuals, our sins and righteous acts will all be judged by God on the day we meet Him face to face. Our position in eternity is based upon our acceptance of Jesus.

Nations will not face God on the day of judgment. Assyria is gone. Babylon is gone. Rome is gone. They have all been weighed and judged in their time. God chose to judge Israel and Judah in their time. Israel is no more and Judah remains as a result of God's judgment and promises. (Today we call Israel what was that remnant of Judah long ago.)

God makes the reasons for judgment very clear. Let us look at those reasons now.

DEFENDING THE DEFENSELESS

21 How the faithful city has become a harlot!
It was full of justice; Righteousness lodged in
it, But now murderers.

22 Your silver has become dross, Your wine
mixed with water.

> 23 Your princes are rebellious, And companions of thieves; Everyone loves bribes, And follows after rewards. They do not defend the fatherless, Nor does the cause of the widow come before them.
>
> Isaiah 1:21-23

God requires leaders and citizens alike to stand up for widows and the fatherless. We are currently a nation of fatherless children. One-third of children in America, to be exact, currently grow up without fathers according to the US Census Bureau. Currently, 40% of all children in America are born to unwed mothers.

We have no shortage of the fatherless, then, so how are we treating them?

A large percentage of prison inmates were in foster care at one point or another. Many prisoners have experienced physical and sexual abuse in their past. In fact, about twenty-five percent of all women[1] and one in seven boys below the age of eighteen in America[2] have experienced some form of abuse.

But does this mean that America has done wrong? Prison is for those who have done wrong, is it not? We lock up the offenders who deserve to be there, right?

Take a recent case that perfectly demonstrates why America has oppressed the fatherless in lieu of bribes and dirty money.

After a recent investigation HSBC, a large international bank, was found to have been knowingly and willfully aiding, abetting and laundering money for international terrorists and Mexican drug/human trafficking cartels.

After the investigation came to light, the United States Justice Department chose to fine HSBC the equivalent of 6 weeks profit instead of pursuing any criminal charges. Why? Their stated reason was that if they filed criminal charges, it could possibly result in HSBC losing banking licenses and then going bankrupt, possibly causing a devastating rift in the financial industry.

The Justice Department in essence declared HSBC and its criminal bankers too big to prosecute.[3]

Because of their money, the bankers proved to be above the law. This does not make those fatherless children rotting in prison innocent, but it clearly shows our nation's willful decision to oppress the fatherless to the benefit of the wealthy.

In 2007, then governor of New York, Eliot Spitzer, was exposed for a scandal involving prostitutes when he was the state's Attorney General and possibly before.[4]

Many believed the reason he was exposed was because when he was Attorney General he chose to prosecute greedy, crooked bankers on Wall Street, where he was also from. There is apparently a culture of prostitution amongst the New York banking industry and a gentlemen's agreement that what goes on in secret after dark stays secret. Angered by Spitzer's prosecution they exposed him for something they were all involved with. Several pimps and madams have claimed that most of the upper level bankers in New York are frequent clients.

Such grotesque revelations make it clear that the wealthy would rather turn the blind eyes of justice on the poor and fatherless than on themselves.

> 14 "When you come to the land which the
> Lord your God is giving you, and possess it
> and dwell in it, and say, 'I will set a king over
> me like all the nations that are around me,'
> 15 you shall surely set a king over you whom
> the Lord your God chooses; one from among
> your brethren you shall set as king over you;
> you may not set a foreigner over you, who is
> not your brother. 16 But he shall not multi-
> ply horses for himself, nor cause the people
> to return to Egypt to multiply horses, for the
> Lord has said to you, 'You shall not return
> that way again.' 17 Neither shall he multiply
> wives for himself, lest his heart turn away;
> nor shall he greatly multiply silver and gold
> for himself. 18 "Also it shall be, when he sits
> on the throne of his kingdom, that he shall
> write for himself a copy of this law in a book,
> from the one before the priests, the Levites.
> 19 And it shall be with him, and he shall
> read it all the days of his life, that he may

> learn to fear the Lord his God and be careful
> to observe all the words of this law and these
> statutes, 20 that his heart may not be lifted
> above his brethren, that he may not turn
> aside from the commandment to the right
> hand or to the left, and that he may prolong
> his days in his kingdom, he and his children
> in the midst of Israel.

Deuteronomy 17:14-20

This passage is talking specifically to kings of Israel and their commitment to God's Law, but several factors are clear. God did not want the leaders of His people amassing great wealth for themselves at the expense of their citizens. In other words, with God's authority He demanded an attitude of servanthood which was exactly the desire of our founding fathers when they established our nation.

Why did God not want the leaders of His people taking all that gold for themselves? Because it would most certainly pervert justice.

The perks of political office in America today are undeniable. Humility and public office are not two qualities we think of together today. We are far from the days when our very wealthy founding fathers chose to limit their power and control over a poor populous.

Our presidents live more lavishly than most kings of history past. Congress grants themselves almost unlimited resources to do as they want as "public servants." The unfathomably large federal bureaucracy now has better paying jobs than private sector equivalents.

When our leaders experience this level of luxury at the expense of the masses, it makes them cold to the plight of those God cares most about--the weak. Not only do we have leaders who care very little for the weak, they use them to maintain their power and control. Many politicians seem happy to use the massive illegal immigration problem we have in the United States as a political bargaining chip to gain the respect of their constituency.

This brings us to another aspect of God's judgment on nations.

HOW WE TREAT FOREIGNERS

God cares deeply how foreigners are treated. First, being a foreigner is hard. It makes you a silent minority with no means of politically or militarily defending yourself. For circumstances often beyond their control, foreigners are almost completely helpless in their host country. That makes them ripe for abuse and oppression.

> The foreigner residing among you must be treated as your native-born. Love them as yourself, for you were foreigners in Egypt. I am the LORD your God.
>
> Leviticus 19:34

At one point or another in the history of the world, every people group was a foreigner to some new place. God cares that we protect and honor foreigners as equal in humanity and value as we honor and value ourselves. As believers, we are always foreigners of this current, temporary realm.

America does not honor or value foreigners as equals anymore. We used to, but sadly those days are over. Today foreigners are political bargaining chips to be used, abused and dealt as treacherously with as anyone can get away with.

Both sides of the political debate claim moral superiority for their position, but it is abundantly clear that neither side is moral on this issue. Nearly all our leaders have used foreigners to their political advantage as best they know how without truly caring about their plight.

TREATMENT OF THE POOR

Much like the issue of how we treat foreigners, God cares deeply about how we treat the poor. Jesus and the apostles made it clear we would have them with us and we needed to care for them (Mark 14:7, Galatians 2:10).

The Old Testament is even more clear. I will list a few here:

Leviticus 19:9-11

9 " 'When you reap the harvest of your land, do not reap to the very edges of your field or gather the gleanings of your harvest. 10 Do not go over your vineyard a second time or pick up the grapes that have fallen. Leave them for the poor and the alien. I am the LORD your God.

Deuteronomy 15:11

11 There will always be poor people in the land. Therefore I command you to be open-handed toward your brothers and toward the poor and needy in your land.

Psalm 82:3-4

3 Defend the cause of the weak and fatherless; maintain the rights of the poor and oppressed. 4 Rescue the weak and needy; deliver them from the hand of the wicked.

Proverbs 14:31

31 He who oppresses the poor shows contempt for their Maker, but whoever is kind to the needy honors God.

Proverbs 19:1

1 Better a poor man whose walk is blameless than a fool whose lips are perverse.

Proverbs 19:17

17 He who is kind to the poor lends to the LORD, and he will reward him for what he has done.

Proverbs 21:13

13 If a man shuts his ears to the cry of the poor, he too will cry out and not be answered.

Proverbs 22:2

2 Rich and poor have this in common: The LORD is the Maker of them all.

Proverbs 29:7

7 The righteous care about justice for the poor, but the wicked have no such concern.

Job 30:25

25 Have I not wept for those in trouble? Has not my soul grieved for the poor?

Isaiah 61:1

1 The Spirit of the Sovereign LORD is on me, because the LORD has anointed me to preach good news to the poor. He has sent me to bind up the brokenhearted, to proclaim freedom for the captives and release from darkness for the prisoners...

Jeremiah 22:16

16 He defended the cause of the poor and needy, and so all went well. Is that not what it means to know me?" declares the LORD.

Zechariah 7:10

10 Do not oppress the widow or the fatherless, the alien or the poor. In your hearts do not think evil of each other.'

In America today, we do not treat the poor well. What is sad is that our nation has one of the best track records in history of caring for the poor. Why? Because up until a generation ago it was almost entirely carried out by church-backed charities.

With so many people existing on government entitlements, it seems counterintuitive to say that our nation does not treat the poor well. There are many in our nation with a deeply held sentiment that our government should support the poor, and it is truly an honorable sentiment. Perhaps all our programs started with the best of intentions, but we are no longer there.

Our programs to care for the poor no longer care for them. Like our foreigners, they are more about political bargaining chips than anything else. In a nation without a declared aristocracy, we have allowed ourselves to create a near-permanent underclass.

Almost every government entitlement program causes its recipients to make a difficult choice. Remain on the program and do little work and barely scrape by well below the poverty level, or take a low paying job and lose all benefits and risk having nothing, still well below the poverty level.

Opportunity still exists in our nation, but our politicians know all too well the barriers they have created. They know that only a small percentage of the population has the necessary willpower and fortitude to escape from the entitlement systems that have been created.

And again, it is not a Democrat or Republican problem. Neither side is willing to reform or cut or make any necessary changes for fear of losing votes and their jobs.

America is a sad bit of horrible irony. In a showy demonstration of "caring for the poor," we actually oppress them. Our programs keep most of them down with the barriers of escape set simply too high for any motivation to change. Our systems encourage poverty, immorality and parental abandonment to name a few.

DOES NOT GOD SEE?

There are so many other ways we could continue on, but it all comes down to our rebellious insistence on self-righteousness. America and God's people have largely turned a blind eye to nearly everything God requires of a nation to be blessed.

I have not even mentioned abortion, human-trafficking, sexual abuse and myriad other horrible realities most people view as too terrible to think about.

This brings us back to God's ability to see. Personally, we can act as if we can sin privately and carry on publicly as if nothing happened, but God sees, and He will judge us when we meet Him for every action. We can, as a nation, act as if we are completely righteous by attempting to redefine righteousness, but the God who sees and judges is not fooled.

God's people must be willing to stand up in this hour. Not as moral guides to the blind, but as the bearers of the Truth we must admit our failure. We must humbly accept the first place of responsibility in our nation's decline. We have held the keys of power and control and have let every manner of evil persist.

No political party, denomination or creed is free from responsibility. Neither is everyone in our nation guilty. There are many voices, from almost every sphere of society, who have remained faithful amidst dark and trying days.

Just like Jesus' words to the church of Sardis in Revelation 3:4, some have not soiled their clothes. We have shining lights in America who have not defiled themselves in the sin and self-righteousness that abounds, and we must encourage those to shine all the brighter.

Because I believe we still have hope. I believe God still has a short window of opportunity for those voices to prevail. God can still grant this nation righteous repentance and leave a blessing instead of a curse.

I have hope, but time is waning...

[1]Dickinson, L., Verloin deGruy, F., Dickinson, W.P., and L. Candib. Health-Related Quality of Life and Symptom Profiles of Female Survivors of Sexual Abuse. Arch Fam Med. 1999;8:35-43.

[2]Delaplane, D. and A. Delaplane. Victims of Child Abuse, Domestic Violence, Elder Abuse, Rape, Robbery, Assault, and Violent Death: A Manual for Clergy and Congregations. Special Edition for Military Chaplains.

[3]Matthew Mosk, ABC News, March 7, 2013. http://abcnews.go.com/Blotter/hsbc-case-senators-prosecu tion-free-zone-big-banks/story?id=18678686#.UW8AQSvS MRk

[4]"Spitzer to step down by Monday". CNN. March 12, 2008. http://www.cnn.com/2008/POLITICS/03/12/spitzer/index. html

Chapter 6
NOW THE GOOD NEWS

The gospel of Jesus Christ does not actually become "good" news without a healthy understanding of the bad news that precedes it. If we do not understand that we are sinners justly condemned to an eternity of punishment and separation from God, then the news of Jesus' sacrifice is just, well, news.

News becomes good news when it is contrasted with something that looks worse. When I was in college I called up my parents after one semester and told them that I had failed three classes, gotten arrested and was being considered for expulsion. When they got over the initial shock, I told them I had made a D in one class. The initial shock (even though they did not buy it) sure made the truth seem a lot better.

The difference in America's situation is that the bad news is real. There is no fabrication needed when we look at scripture and history. God will judge a wicked and rebellious nation that is filled with innocent blood, corruption and repression. Our bad news is very real. Our good news is also very real, but we must choose to accept it.

The good news in our situation is that America does not have to continue to go the wrong way. The great news in our situation, I believe, is that we do not even have to change any laws or lobby for policy change. The good news will come as a result of repentance on the part of God's people.

THE POWER OF REPENTANCE

If we repent, God may just relent from His righteous judgment over our nation.

> If my people, who are called by my name,
> will humble themselves and pray and seek
> my face and turn from their wicked ways,
> then will I hear from heaven and will forgive
> their sin and will heal their land.
>
> 2 Chronicles 7:14

The key part of this verse is "my people." God is not requiring us to legislate morality on the part of the lost in our nation. He is requiring "His people" to repent. If God's people will repent of our wicked ways, then God will turn aside from His judgment and heal our land. He will leave a blessing instead of a curse.

> 12 "Now, therefore," says the Lord, "Turn to
> Me with all your heart, with fasting, with
> weeping, and with mourning." 13 So rend
> your heart, and not your garments; Return to

the Lord your God, For He is gracious and merciful, Slow to anger, and of great kindness; And He relents from doing harm.

14 Who knows if He will turn and relent, And leave a blessing behind Him—A grain offering and a drink offering For the Lord your God?

15 Blow the trumpet in Zion, Consecrate a fast, Call a sacred assembly;

16 Gather the people, Sanctify the congregation, Assemble the elders, Gather the children and nursing babes; Let the bridegroom go out from his chamber, And the bride from her dressing room.

Joel 2:12-16

The good news in America's situation is there is still time for God to leave a blessing instead of a curse. God is gracious and compassionate, slow to anger and abounding in love. Moses' statement is very important for us today:

18 'The LORD is slow to anger and abundant in lovingkindness, forgiving iniquity and transgression; but He will by no means clear the guilty, visiting the iniquity of the fathers on the children to the third and the fourth generations.' 19 "Pardon, I pray, the iniquity of this people according to the greatness of Your lovingkindness, just as You also have

> forgiven this people, from Egypt even until
> now."
>
> Numbers 14:18-19

God will not leave the guilty unpunished, but He is patient. He is slow to anger. God is longing to release a blessing over America, but He will only do it on His terms.

We in America have become so familiar with the "grace of God" message that we often forget the very nature of our relationship to Him. We must remember that we are the created and He is the creator. We do not make the rules. We do not get to bend them. We can only play by God's set of rules. Paul says it well in Romans:

> Therefore consider the goodness and severity
> of God: on those who fell, severity; but to-
> ward you, goodness, if you continue in His
> goodness. Otherwise you also will be cut off.
>
> Romans 11:22

GOD'S GRACE

We must realize that God longs to be gracious to us, but He requires that we do things His way. We do not get to live however we want and expect God to bless us. His grace is not bestowed upon us without adherence to His ways. It is a confusing concept for many in the church today. For many, the question is,

"Is God's grace free or are there requirements we must meet to receive it?"

The answer is both, from our perspective. We cannot do anything to earn God's grace. It is very much a free gift, but at the same time, we must repent, change our lives and strive to live according to God's ways. Our reality seems quite paradoxical. This has been the challenge of theologians for centuries trying to understand this.

There is nothing we can do to earn God's grace, but He does tell us plainly that we must play by His rules if we want to walk in it. That is true on a personal level as well as a societal (corporate) level.

We must not be so foolish to think that our nation will continue to receive God's grace and blessing if we choose to live contrary to how God requires. We cannot claim God but live contrary to who He is. If we do return to Him "with all our hearts" He may just leave a blessing behind. We certainly do not deserve a blessing just for repenting, but that is where God's grace is free. We cannot earn it, but if we choose to obey Him He will grant it to us.

America's greatest days may still be ahead, but it will take resolve on the part of God's people, the church. At this point in time I believe we have two vastly different possible outcomes. One outcome will be the result of changing nothing; the other will be a result of changing everything.

So what will repentance look like? What must the church do to receive this blessing from God? What are the practical steps we must take to see God relent from His anger over our nation and the injustices we have perpetrated?

PERSONAL REPENTANCE

What is at stake in America is not really personal judgment but corporate judgment. Individually, we will all stand before the Lord one day and face judgment. If we believe in Jesus, we will be judged righteous and enter into eternity with God. Then our actions here on earth will be judged and we will be rewarded accordingly.

America will not stand before God on the day of Judgment. It stands for its judgment now and America will rise and fall based on how it responds to the challenges it faces today. But America is not just a flag or a bald eagle on a quarter. It is made up of people. Millions of them. America's outcome before the court of heaven depends on how individuals respond.

That brings us to personal repentance. America cannot repent corporately without individual repentance. The nation must have leaders humble enough to take the first step to bow low before the Lord. By leaders, I do not mean the president and congress. I mean people who are willing to take the lead in repenting themselves and calling others to repentance.

Pastors, teachers, plumbers, engineers, writers, attorneys, carpenters, doctors, janitors, secretaries, CEOs and electricians can all be the leaders we need to take that first step. We can be so paralyzed by fear of stepping out, hoping that a true leader will emerge, that we never take that first step.

God is not asking for leaders to take the first step toward leading this nation down the right path, but He is asking for anyone to lead who is willing. Look at what scripture says:

> 26 Brothers and sisters, think of what you were when you were called. Not many of you were wise by human standards; not many were influential; not many were of noble birth. 27 But God chose the foolish things of the world to shame the wise; God chose the weak things of the world to shame the strong. 28 God chose the lowly things of this world and the despised things—and the things that are not—to nullify the things that are, 29 so that no one may boast before him. 30 It is because of him that you are in Christ Jesus, who has become for us wisdom from God—that is, our righteousness, holiness and redemption.
>
> 1 Corinthians 1:26-30

God has not chosen the wise, the rich or the powerful to lead His kingdom. He has chosen those He knows will say yes. He has chosen those with a humble heart who know it is not their own abilities but God's that makes the difference. God is not looking for influential people to change our nation, but for humble people who will rely on His influence to change us.

That all starts with our own personal willingness to repent. Will we choose to follow God with all our hearts before we try or expect anyone else to?

Are you trapped in pornography? Greed? Theft? Gambling? Drugs and alcohol? Abuse? Self-righteousness? Living for yourself? Go to God and ask for help. Repent of your sin and ask Him for help to overcome them. Make restitution for the things you have stolen from others and do what you need to restore relationships.

Zacchaeus was so overwhelmed by the grace and forgiveness he experienced from Jesus that he could not think of doing anything but an extravagant act of repentance.

> But Zacchaeus stood up and said to the
> Lord, "Look, Lord! Here and now I give half
> of my possessions to the poor, and if I have
> cheated anybody out of anything, I will pay
> back four times the amount."

Luke 19:8

Will you be so overcome by the reality of Jesus' forgiveness of your sins that you will humble yourself to repentance? Do you have too much to lose by admitting you have sinned? Consider the eternity that God has offered to us. This life is unthinkably short in comparison to eternity with God. Nothing else makes sense now but to live for eternity. What little respect, honor and dignity we have now will be gone in just a moment, and we will stand before a loving and righteous God. In that hour we will consider every act of repentance and humility the wisest decision of our life.

CORPORATE REPENTANCE

One of the amazing things about God is how He rewards. All men and women seek honor, dignity, respect and even fame. We long for greatness. That may look different for each of us, but the longing is in us all. It is not sinful because God put it in us. He longs to reward us for eternity. He wants us great forever.

What makes that longing sinful is when we try to fulfill it with illicit desires. It is hard for us humans to rightly see eternity and change our lives now based on it, but that is what God is asking of us. We can seek our own glory and honor here on earth, but we have no power to earn glory and honor in eternity. Only God can grant that.

What is amazing is that God also has the power to give to us honor and respect in this life, too. We fight and claw our way to the "top" in this life, but it is all futility. Only God has the authority to give us respect, honor, dignity, authority and greatness in eternity *and* this age.

That means there is nothing else that makes sense for us as a nation but to humble ourselves and return to the Lord. That kind of repentance will start with the ones who choose to personally repent. It will become contagious when others see the power of God on their lives.

The power of God is not just in miracles, signs and wonders (although those are great). The true power of God as experienced by people in this life is the ability to transform us from self-seeking sinners into eternally-focused lovers of God. Miracles, signs and wonders are powerful, but nothing changes a people like the stirrings of revival.

As more and more people bow their hearts low before the Lord, they feel the cleansing power of His blood, love and forgiveness. That is a fire that spreads faster than in any forest because people are so hungry to see real change. Real love. Real joy. Real peace.

Our personal repentance will not stay personal. As we seek God's face with more and more energy, our lives will become contagious. Others will want what we have.

We need revival that can only come from God, but amazingly He only stirs hearts through partnership with us. When one person humbles himself before God, it makes two others jealous for the same freedom. When those two humble themselves, it makes four more hungry for the same cleansing of their hearts. Then eight turn into 16 and 16 into 32 and before long you have a massive stirring of souls turning to the Lord.

Nothing spreads faster than hearts truly energized by the love and forgiveness of Jesus. That kind of revival does not take long before it affects a nation.

But it has to start with you. We cannot wait for three other people to repent and humble themselves and return to the Lord. We have to risk looking foolish. We have to risk seeming less "holy." We have to give up our right to having everyone think we are put together.

Do you want to see America repent and be blessed by God? It does not start with the president, congress or even your pastor; it starts with you.

START HERE

People are not stupid. They have seen Christians call everyone else to repentance for decades now without seeing any true change in us. We cannot fake repentance. Not before God and not even before others. The only ones we truly deceive are ourselves.

America has seen the repentance and call to righteous living we have offered them and they have issued a collective "no." Christians have almost completely lost the culture that was ours to influence because no one sees anything different in us than in themselves.

People are smart enough to spot the phony calls for morality we have given them, but they are also powerless but to acknowledge true change when they see it. America is not a stubborn nation refusing to turn to the Lord. Our nation is hungry to see God move here, but it has been decades since we have seen it.

The revival and awakening America needs will start with God's people. Are we willing to turn our calls for morality in on ourselves? Are we willing to silence our attempts to legislate others' lives and first start living wholly for God ourselves?

A simple message of hope backed by the power of God's love on our lives will transform our nation. It has changed the course of history for two thousand years, and it is still what we need today.

> 1 And so it was with me, brothers and sisters. When I came to you, I did not come with eloquence or human wisdom as I proclaimed to you the testimony about God. 2 For I resolved to know nothing while I was with you except Jesus Christ and him crucified. 3 I came to you in weakness with great fear and trembling. 4 My message and my preaching

were not with wise and persuasive words,
but with a demonstration of the Spirit's
power, 5 so that your faith might not rest on
human wisdom, but on God's power.

1 Corinthians 2:1-5

Chapter 7
TIME IS SHORT

I do not want to stir up fear, but I do want to sound a clear alarm. No one is ever angry at a fire alarm for rudely awakening them up in the middle of the night and saving their lives from a fire. In the same way I want to be as an alarm that awakens our nation before our house is consumed with the smoke and fire that will destroy us.

An alarm is designed to sound when there is immediate danger. "Get out now!" is the clear message. But when the alarm goes off every time we burn toast, it begins to dull our senses to the danger that the alarm is designed to save us from. The same can be true when we speak of the judgment of God.

Be honest: when I say "judgment of God" do you immediately imagine a man wearing a sandwich board with "The End Is Near" written across it? Do you picture a man on television talking about how bad America is and that he hopes we are judged for our sins? Most Americans have been dulled to the idea of impending judgment because we have been overrun with the concept for decades. Some people have even removed the very concept of the judgment of God from their theology because they are so tired of the "false alarms."

MICROWAVE GENERATION

We are truly a people who cannot wait for anything. Immediate gratification is apparent in our debt problems, our growing waistlines from eating out and the housing bubble of years past. We want results now and our minds struggle with answers that are not immediate.

Each year we grow more accustomed to the idea of "if it did not happen recently, it does not matter." News story cycles are most often dead after a week and the idea that a patient God would warn us months, years or decades in advance is a foreign concept.

Our culture has speculated that such warnings of judgment from years past are merely burned toast. No real danger exists because nothing has happened yet. We are still here and we are still doing fine. The doomsday prophets are just blowing smoke.

I do not want to stand in defense of every want-to-be doomsday prophet out there. In fact, I think a very effective strategy of the enemy is to flood us with an overabundance of two very opposite voices. One is the voice that says God hates us and will judge us for our sins. The second is the one that proclaims God loves us so He cannot judge us. Both are partially true and mostly false. God does not hate us; He loves us. It is because He loves us that He will chasten us. That chastening will come in the form of judgment. God will stand up for those who are crying out from oppression, murder and all the other evils that befall them.

The truth is that God loves us too much to let us continue to stray forever. He will bring judgment on us to refine and purify us *because* He loves us.

UNDERSTANDING TIMING

If God has truly been telling us for decades that judgment is coming but has not acted yet, how do we know when it is too late?

The simple answer is we do not. We do not know when God will truly bring judgment, but that is not really the right question to be asking. It seems to be the question we are most concerned with, however.

"How long can we keep on sinning as we are before we have to repent to avert judgment?" is the sentiment many seem to espouse. Nothing could be further from the heart of God or more disastrous for our nation.

The correct attitude would be to say, "God, what must we do *today* to prevent judgment from coming? How long will You delay so that we can labor in fasting and prayer and weeping for our nation and people?"

Knowing the timing of the Lord is very difficult because He does not often share that information with us. Sometimes God gives dates and timeframes, but those are exceptions, not the rule. When God says "change," the implication is always "now."

Sometimes it may be that God's timing is dynamic. Our response may determine the speed at which God acts. He may delay if we make some of the changes He asks for.

Then again, if we get worse, God may judge us more quickly. If we repent a little, God may stay His hand for a little more time. What that means to us is that we should not be trying to milk God's timing for all the sin we can, but that we should be using what little time we have to pray for radical transformation of our church, family, friends and culture. Now is the time to pray and fast, not to debate whether God is truly just to judge us for our sins.

TIME IS TRULY SHORT

I am not willing to simply hope that God will stay His hand if we respond a little. I believe He has already done this a few times. I want to sound an alarm clearly and loudly enough to awaken my Christian brothers and sisters to prayer, fasting and action. We must first change ourselves and that will only happen by sounding the alarm.

I have already told you why I believe the time is short. God showed me that the completed One World Trade Center building would be a "sign and seal" of His coming judgment. I do not know if that means God will immediately judge us once the building is finished or if He just means that once it is finished it will stand for the judgment to come.

I also do not know when the building will be "completed" in God's mind. Construction completion? First tenants moving in? Full occupancy? I hope for the latest possible dates, but I am not willing to rest on that. No matter how you view it, the building will be complete much too soon.

What I am saying is I do not know what the day and hour is that we cannot turn back from. A point of no return exists, but God has not shared that with me, or anyone else I know or have heard for that matter. But I am frightened to think about it that way. I want to call the church to repentance, prayer and fasting now before that building is finished, and I know what a logistical challenge that is.

Time is very short before that building will be done and I feel the urgency to call for repentance. You may actually be reading this after it has been finished.

What then?

Repent anyway. Call your friends, family and church to turn with all their hearts to God. It is never too late to turn your heart toward God, but it may be too late to receive the full blessing He longs to give us.

WHO KNOWS?

Joel uses a very strange phrase while encouraging repentance. "Who knows if He will turn and relent, and leave a blessing behind Him?" (Joel 2:14) That "who knows" is a very interesting way to phrase the statement. Should not the prophet who is calling for repentance directly from God know whether or not God will relent?

His problem was the same we face today. Depending on when you are reading this, it may already be too late. God has not shared with us when the point of no return is just like He did not share it with Joel. There was no date written in stone, nor is there today. There are alarms along the way warning us of the coming day of judgment, but often we do not know when the point of no return is until it is already too apparent to do anything about it.

The fact that God shared an apparent timing with me in my dream is troubling, but I still cannot tell you a date. I just know it is close.

THE POINT OF NO RETURN

Jeremiah experienced this point of no return only after it was too late. "Do not pray for this people or offer any plea or petition for them, because I will not listen when they call to me in the time of their distress." (Jeremiah 11:14)

Obviously it was too late for Judah at this point, but I believe it is not too late for us and I do not want to wait until it is. If you are reading this and it has become too late, do not despair. There is hope yet, but the best options for us would have already come and gone.

In Chapters 7-9 I present three very different responses to God's coming judgment and how to find God's favor in each, even if it is too late for God to relent from judgment.

God will always be slow to anger, abounding in love for those who turn to Him. Even if you are reading this and America is under judgment, do not lose hope. Press into God anyway and maybe God will lighten our load. Maybe He will yet bless us anyway.

I choose to never give up hope that God will return to us and bless us. Even when One World Trade Center is complete, I will not give up hope that God will relent. I will, however, have less faith we will get out of this without some pain once that day comes and goes. What I will not do is stop praying, fasting and crying out for God to heal us.

Do not wait for the day of no return. Do not even bother asking God when that might be. Commit yourself to personal repentance, prayer and fasting. Commit to purity, holiness and devotion to God. Not in an attempt to earn God's favor but as the only logical response to God's great mercy and grace over your life through His sacrifice on the cross.

THE CROSS: ALWAYS OUR ONLY RESPONSE

In the end, God will not judge or relent based on our ability to stop sinning. Bad behavior will not be our undoing. God will judge us based on whether or not His people are leaning on Him or on themselves. If we are leaning on Him, then we know there is nothing we can do to earn His favor; we can only rest our hope on the finished work of the cross.

When we try to be good in our own strength, we always end up failing. When we give up our attempt to "be good" and instead trust in God's grace to purify us, only then do we have hope. Our response to God's warning of judgment is no different than what our response should always be. We should be content to "know nothing but Christ crucified," (1 Corinthians 2:2).

Jesus' work on the cross has always and will always be our only hope. No amount of good behavior will change God's mind about us. Only acknowledgement of our sin and confession of our reliance on God will change us, our nation and God's mind.

Now is the time to repent. Now is the time to change. Now is the time to throw ourselves upon the mercy of the cross and earnestly and honestly ask for God's forgiveness and help.

It is not too late, but it will be soon.

Chapter 8
SODOM AND GOMORRAH
A Case Study of Judgment

Sodom is a name associated with every kind of evil imaginable. When people hear the word, they almost universally think of the harsh judgment of God. In scripture it stands as one of the foremost symbols of God's judgment after the flood itself.

What can we learn from Sodom and Gomorrah? Why did God judge them? What standard does God use when judging men, and why was this case so harsh? Is He indiscriminate or is there a method to what many perceive as madness?

First, let us look at what God judges and what He does not.

God judges on behalf of men (and women); He does not judge sin. That may sound strange, but if God judged a nation's sin, not a day would go by without the strict judgment of God. Many people today have this notion that "God hates the sin but not the sinner." This phrase is rooted in a little truth, but it does more harm than good to our understanding of God's judgment.

Let us use our justice system as an example to learn from. A jury is chosen to determine the facts of a case. They are never appointed to determine if someone broke the law, but to determine what exactly a person did and did not do. Whether a law was broken is up to the prosecutor and judge. Since jurors are not experts in the law, their task is simple and clearcut: determine what someone did and report on that. The prosecutor informs the jury whether or not a law was broken and to what degree.

In the same way, God does not judge sin in this age; sin is the measuring stick He uses in the court case against nations. He does not judge the sin, but He uses it to proclaim judgment against a guilty party. In the same way, a court does not hand down a judgment against murder or theft; they hand down a judgment against some person who has murdered or stolen. Right now, God judges men, not sin.

What gets confusing when we talk about "God hates sin, not sinners" is that we assume that God does not judge sinners but that He judges their sin. This is not possible! Again, it is like saying God hates murder but He is totally okay with murderers. He is not and it would be very difficult to say He was a good judge if He was!

We know that God will ultimately judge all sin as well. Everything defined as evil, God will judge at the end of this age. Paul tells us that death will be the last thing He will judge (1 Corinthians 15:26), and it will be done away with forever. In this way God *will* judge sin, but that will only happen once and for all at the end of time. For our purposes now, God is still using sin as a litmus test and as we will see, the only reason He will ultimately judge sin is because Jesus paid the price for its eventual judgment.

HOW DOES GOD JUDGE?

Until that day of final judgment, we exist in this temporal age where God judges men. But how does He judge? Why does He judge some men and not others?

The psalmists ask this question many times:

> How long will you defend the unjust and
> show partiality to the wicked?
>
> Psalm 82:2

> 1 O Lord, the God who avenges, O God who
> avenges, shine forth.
>
> 2 Rise up, O Judge of the earth; pay back to
> the proud what they deserve.
>
> 3 How long will the wicked, O Lord, how
> long will the wicked be jubilant?

4 They pour out arrogant words; all the evil-doers are full of boasting.

5 They crush your people, O Lord; they oppress your inheritance.

6 They slay the widow and the alien; they murder the fatherless.

7 They say, "The Lord does not see; the God of Jacob pays no heed."

Psalm 94:1-7

The psalmists were just as perplexed by God's judgment of some men and not others, so we find ourselves in good company asking such questions. It will help us if we come up with the same conclusions as they did.

8 Take heed, you senseless ones among the people; you fools, when will you become wise?

9 Does he who implanted the ear not hear? Does he who formed the eye not see?

10 Does he who disciplines nations not punish? Does he who teaches man lack knowledge?

Psalm 94:8-10

God judges for just what we think He does: evil. He judges wrongdoers for their sins, but there is a catch. God is patient. God waits to judge sin. He restrains Himself from casting judgment until the moment He deems it the most necessary.

Any illustration will fall helplessly short of understanding God's perfect judgment and timing, but one fits well for me. Consider an FBI agent tracking a low-level drug dealer. If the FBI arrests the drug dealer and takes him off the street, there will be four more ready to take his place. The FBI knows that they have to catch the higher-level traffickers to do any good.

Instead of arresting the low-level drug pushers, detectives watch and wait for them to inadvertently give up information on their higher-ups. They patiently wait for the opportunity to take down an entire criminal organization. They know the real prize is to eliminate the leaders of an organization, so they wait for their opportunities.

God is something like this if we are to use a human example. God has patience for man's sin so that He may bring the most justice for the most people in His timing. Will He at times appear unjust to some? Definitely. Does that mean God is unjust? Certainly not!

God's Forbearance

God waits patiently. He gives men opportunities to repent and turn to Him. He actually lets men hurt, abuse and even kill others in His patience. Why He protects and preserves some and not others is a mystery for the ages we will only fully understand in eternity, but His patience seems to allow that some fall victim to wicked men.

But we see clearly the limit to God's patience in Sodom and Gomorrah. There comes a time where God will no longer be patient with those who break His righteous decrees. There comes a day where God will not turn away from sinful men.

Cries from the abused, murdered and wounded filled God's ears from Sodom and Gomorrah. God Himself, in some manifestation, pays Abraham a visit along with two angels He intended to send on to Sodom and makes his plans known. God sends the two angels on their way to Sodom, and Abraham famously pleads with God for Sodom's salvation. The exchange is very interesting.

> 24 What if there are fifty righteous people in the city? Will you really sweep it away and not spare the place for the sake of the fifty righteous people in it? 25 Far be it from you to do such a thing—to kill the righteous with the wicked, treating the righteous and the wicked alike. Far be it from you! Will not the Judge of all the earth do right?"
>
> 26 The Lord said, "If I find fifty righteous people in the city of Sodom, I will spare the whole place for their sake."

27 Then Abraham spoke up again: "Now that I have been so bold as to speak to the Lord, though I am nothing but dust and ashes, 28 what if the number of the righteous is five less than fifty? Will you destroy the whole city because of five people?"

"If I find forty-five there," he said, "I will not destroy it."

29 Once again he spoke to him, "What if only forty are found there?"

He said, "For the sake of forty, I will not do it."

30 Then he said, "May the Lord not be angry, but let me speak. What if only thirty can be found there?"

He answered, "I will not do it if I find thirty there."

31 Abraham said, "Now that I have been so bold as to speak to the Lord, what if only twenty can be found there?"

He said, "For the sake of twenty, I will not destroy it."

32 Then he said, "May the Lord not be angry, but let me speak just once more. What if only ten can be found there?"

He answered, "For the sake of ten, I will not destroy it."

> 33 When the Lord had finished speaking
> with Abraham, he left, and Abraham re-
> turned home.

> Genesis 18:24-33

Abraham obviously knew just how bad Sodom was. After all, he had rescued Lot and all the people of Sodom when they were attacked and carried away by an invading army. Abraham knew then that Sodom was evil because he would not accept a dime from the king of Sodom (Genesis 14:21-24).

If only ten people were righteous, God would have spared Sodom and Gomorrah. What does He mean by righteous? He is not saying people who do not sin, because there is no such person. All throughout scripture a righteous person is one who follows God with all their heart and tries to do His will. Someone who sins but turns to the Lord is considered righteous. Someone who refuses to repent of their sin and turn to God is considered unrighteous and wicked.

> 16 For though a righteous man falls seven
> times, he rises again, but the wicked are
> brought down by calamity.

> Proverbs 24:16

So God's standard for saving Sodom is not ten perfect people but just ten people who will acknowledge their sin and turn back to God. Just ten people who will call sin sin and look to God. Obviously Abraham was worried that there were not actually ten but he apparently did not dare ask God down any more than that.

We find out in Genesis chapter 19 that there were not ten righteous people. It is hard to believe that even Lot was considered righteous, but God exonerates him, albeit in a very sad way.

> 7 and if he rescued Lot, a righteous man, who was distressed by the depraved conduct of the lawless 8 (for that righteous man, living among them day after day, was tormented in his righteous soul by the lawless deeds he saw and heard)
>
> 2 Peter 2:7-8

We find in Genesis 19:1 that Lot was sitting at the city gate. In ancient times that meant he was a judge over the city. People would bring their disputes to the judge that sat at the city gate. He probably got that job as a thank-you for his uncle, Abraham, saving the entire city. But obviously under Lot's watch Sodom's sin had escalated and reached God's ears as "grievous" (Genesis 18:20).

When the residents of Sodom tried to forcefully take the two angels away from Lot to rape them, Lot offered his daughters to them instead. That is not exactly the kind of action I would expect from "father of the year" but God declared Lot righteous anyway. The sad thing is that he was not strong enough in character to lead the city a different way even though he was their judge.

TOTAL CORRUPTION

The city of Sodom was so wicked that there were not ten people God could spare the place on behalf of. What is interesting is that God sent two angels to enter Sodom to see if their sin was as bad as God had heard. Did God not already know that? Did God need to send the angels? Obviously not, but He did anyway to prove Himself to Abraham, Lot and the residents of Sodom and Gomorrah that He was a righteous judge.

God's decrees are timeless. "On the testimony of two or three witnesses a man shall be put to death" (Deuteronomy 17:6). Even though He had not yet given this law, it still existed in the knowledge of God. He sent the angels to prove beyond a shadow of doubt that the residents of Sodom and Gomorrah all deserved death. God proved they were deserving of His judgment.

That judgment was to shortly come as fire from heaven. The entire valley that contained the two cities of Sodom and Gomorrah was completely consumed by fire. Besides the flood and a few other occasions where angels bring death, this is the only other judgment in the Old Testament where God supernaturally and directly judges the people of earth. Every other judgment will be through the sword, famine and disease.

GOD'S JUDGMENTS ARE RIGHTEOUS

We need to consider several points from the story of God's judgment of Sodom and Gomorrah. First and foremost is that God's judgments are righteous. This is God's first "big" judgment post-flood against the people on earth. Even though He does not owe us any explanation, God went to great lengths to prove that He was righteous in His judgment of Sodom.

God's judgments offend the sinful heart of man. We find in Revelation that God sends judgment upon the inhabitants of earth. Their reaction is not only to acknowledge that they know God Himself is carrying them out but to blaspheme His name. God will expose the wickedness of man in that day when He sends judgment on earth to try and turn the hearts of men back to Himself and they instead resist and hate Him for it (Revelation 16:21).

A sovereign God does not owe us any answers for His actions. He made us. He makes the rules. But we find out that we are incapable of following those rules so we need redemption. We need restoration. We need forgiveness. In all His dealings God is "slow to anger, abounding in love and forgiving sin and rebellion. Yet he does not leave the guilty unpunished; he punishes the children for the sin of the fathers to the third and fourth generation" (Numbers 14:18).

God is faithful to forgive those who seek Him for forgiveness. That is why He does not punish sin on the spot. We all suffer from the sins of others, not because God is not just, but because He is patient. In the end, though, God judges the sins of the unrepentant. He carries out His righteous vengeance on behalf of those who have been wounded, hurt, abused, murdered, cheated and oppressed. God sees and hears, and even though He may wait for a time, He always gives justice to those who cry out for it. And He is always righteous in His judgments.

> 5 Then I heard the angel in charge of the waters say: "You are just in these judgments, you who are and who were, the Holy One, because you have so judged;
>
> 6 for they have shed the blood of your saints and prophets, and you have given them blood to drink as they deserve."
>
> 7 And I heard the altar respond: "Yes, Lord God Almighty, true and just are your judgments."
>
> Revelation 16:5-7

ABRAHAM'S BARGAINING

Will God give us the same deal He gave Abraham? Will He turn aside from judgment against America if there are ten righteous people? I do not think God will turn aside for ten people, just based on numbers. There certainly were not 320 million people in Sodom and Gomorrah, but what is God's threshold for America? Will He spare us if ten percent of His people cry out in repentance? What if five percent cry out? Or even one percent?

God will be just in His judgment against America if He does in fact send it. We have murdered millions of innocents through abortion. We have abused millions of children. We have trafficked sexual slaves. We exported sexual insanity around the world through pornography. We have politicians who have perverted justice through bribes. We have pastors and leaders who have spoken lies and led people astray out of greed (Micah 3:11, 2 Peter 2:14).

If we are honest with our position before God, we must acknowledge that God would be just in judging America. The divorce rate, the abortion rate, the infidelity rate and the drug and crime rate are identical inside and outside the church. As believers we must agree with God's judgment upon America. There is no other righteous position but to agree with God that we deserve His immediate judgment upon our nation for our wickedness.

The real question for us is not whether we rightly deserve judgment, but whether or not God will relent. Will God relent if just one percent of His people cry out in repentance and return to Him with all their hearts?

> "If my people, who are called by my name,
> will humble themselves and pray and seek
> my face and turn from their wicked ways,
> then will I hear from heaven and will forgive
> their sin and will heal their land."

2 Chronicles 7:14

We do not know. I believe my dream is a warning because we still have time to repent. We still have an opportunity to change our ways. And as we see in Sodom and Gomorrah, it is not up to us to change our nation to avoid judgment, but just to find enough righteous souls to turn back to God so that He will spare the nation on our behalf.

I do not believe that has happened yet. God has set a timetable based on a building in New York before He pronounces His righteous judgment against us. We still have hope. The church still has an opportunity to change. We can still plead with God to spare us.

Will we find enough people to turn God's judgments away?

Lord, have mercy on us. Raise up our "ten righteous" for which you will relent.

Chapter 9
NINEVEH
A Case Study of Judgment

What happens when judgment is pronounced, and unlike in Sodom and Gomorrah, the people turn? What happens when people repent and return to God? Does He spare them or does He carry out His judgment against them anyway?

The book of Jonah gives us our answer. God pronounced judgment against Assyria's capital of Nineveh and then relented when the entire city repented. But to fully understand what happened in Nineveh, it is helpful to have a little background knowledge for the book of Jonah.

GOD'S RELUCTANT PROPHET
As we read the book of Jonah we clearly see that Jonah wanted nothing to do with Nineveh being spared God's judgment. Jonah seems to have been happy with the idea of the entire city going to hell for

eternity with no remorse. What would cause a prophet of God to be so hateful against a lost people?

Many have said that Jonah was simply prejudiced against the people of Nineveh. They were a race of Gentiles and Jonah hated them because they were not Hebrew. Whereas Jonah may have actually had a superiority complex about his own people, it is clear from scripture this was not Jonah's reservation.

Jonah hated the people of Nineveh so much that he did not want to go and warn them of God's coming judgment. Jonah knew that God is slow to anger and abounding in love. Jonah's true fear was not that they would kill him for his message, but that they would actually turn and God would spare the people of Nineveh. Jonah knew God well enough to know He would forgive them and he wanted no part of offering the people of Nineveh hope. If it was not simple racial prejudice, what could it have been that so soured Jonah to the people of Nineveh?

I think the only way an American could understand Jonah's mental state is if we use a little hypothetical situation.

A LITTLE HYPOTHETICAL

Picture that instead of the United States pounding Afghanistan "back to the stone age" after the 9/11 attacks, that we actually encountered an enemy up to the challenge of beating us. What if instead of winning in Afghanistan, we lost the war on terror? What if they had been so well-prepared and well-equipped that they had beaten us in Afghanistan and then brought the fight to America's shores?

Imagine for a moment that has happened. 2012 was not a typical year of presidential debates here in America but a year of rebuilding after Al-Qaeda devastated our infrastructure from years of successive wars. They had gone for now, but ten years of Al-Qaeda barraging our cities with bombs left our great buildings in rubble. Our proud monuments are destroyed. Our great cities lie in ruin and our pride is all gone. Half of all Americans have either been killed in the fighting or carried away overseas to work for their new Al-Qaeda overlords.

Imagine that your parents, half of your cousins and one of your children died in the fighting. Somehow you survived, but your spirit has been crushed and moving forward seems impossible. Life has forever changed from the peace and safety you once enjoyed and everywhere you go in your town there is still leftover destruction. And on top of that, the threat of Al Qaida attacking again is still there.

Now, picture the Lord standing in front of you and calling you to take a mission trip to Afghanistan to tell them that if they would repent, God would spare them from destruction. You would probably not be too keen on offering salvation to the people who chose not to spare you.

That is how we should understand the story of Jonah.

THE CRANKY PROPHET

Assyria fought against Israel for decades and eventually became the end of them. Jonah had a good reason to hold on to hatred and bitterness toward the Assyrians (not that he should have). It is probably likely that when he eventually did walk through Nineveh he encountered slaves of his own people being held there. The entire affair was one shrouded in terrible pain for Jonah.

We should be slow to judge Jonah for what he did. He decided that if the Ninevites could not hear God's warning, they would certainly be wiped out and that was just fine by him. Jonah ran the other way and boarded a ship to sail across the Mediterranean. Maybe Jonah thought that if he could get as far away from Nineveh, God would have a harder time forcing him to go there. He knew that God had Joseph kidnapped to take him to Egypt so maybe Jonah thought God could not catch him at sea. Whatever the reason, we see clearly that Jonah was running the opposite direction as fast as he could in an effort to doom the Assyrians.

We actually have quite a bit of this going on in the United States. We have tons of "cranky prophets." Every day one political party has control of our nation we are barraged through the media with scare tactics of just how bad things are now and how bad things are going to be if their political party does not regain control. We are doomed just because the other party is in power. If the Democrats are in control, then the nation is falling apart, according to Republicans. Ten minutes after the Republicans take control back the nation has never been better. It is the same story for the Democrats.

This may not sound very spiritual relating our national politics to stories from the Bible, but I am confident that most people who consider themselves Christian in our nation know more about the current struggles between Republicans and Democrats than they do about almost any story in scripture. Believers are just sure that it is the "other side" that is causing the demise of our nation. The problem is that if God judges our nation, it will be because He did not find enough people to repent, not because one "side" chose not to see things our way. We will all suffer and we will all be responsible.

Christians must remove themselves from the political fray we have found ourselves in if we are to overcome this. I am not advocating that Christians stop engaging in politics; I think our nation would be much worse off without us in the political arena. No, I am advocating that Christians start acting as citizens of God's Kingdom before America. We really can have both, but only if we "seek first the kingdom of God" (Matthew 6:33).

But there is a better way. In fact, there is only one way.

REPENTANCE

If you are not familiar with the story of Jonah, I would encourage you to read the whole book right now. It is not long. Many people are familiar with his story from Sunday school and children's Bible stories. Jonah boarded a ship and set sail to anywhere he could find that was not Nineveh. God sent a storm so bad that the sailors asked God if there was someone on board who was causing it and they learned it was Jonah. Jonah admitted he knew it was his fault and if they threw him overboard they would live.

Jonah may not have known God would spare his life, but He had the most interesting rescue in store for Jonah. Some kind of giant fish swallowed Jonah where he spent the next three days in complete darkness, probably struggling to breathe with a stench that no human should ever have to experience.

The time in the fish's belly would later come to be a prophetic symbol of Jesus' time in the grave before His resurrection. Just like the Messiah to come, Jonah was "resurrected" when he called out to God and God had the fish, quite conveniently, throw him up on the shore of the Mediterranean.

The Lord again told Jonah to proclaim His warning against Nineveh and this time Jonah obeyed. Nineveh was so large it took three days to tour--a gargantuan city of antiquity. Jonah proclaimed his message of doom and gloom, wrath and destruction all over the city. News of Jonah's message began to spread throughout the city and a very strange thing happened. The people of Nineveh began to fast for the mercy of God.

When the news reached the king of Assyria, he declared a national corporate fast of repentance. He required everyone to turn from "their evil ways and their violence" (Jonah 3:8). The king thought, "Who knows? God may yet relent and with compassion turn from his fierce anger so that we will not perish" (Jonah 3:9).

And God did just that. He saw the people of Nineveh's honest repentance, and He withheld His hand of judgment against them. The magnitude of that event probably still resounds throughout heaven to this day. A pagan nation listened to the very cranky voice of a Hebrew prophet who was giddy to see them destroyed. Instead of killing Jonah, they listened and turned.

This is what Jonah was afraid of from the beginning.

GOD'S MESSAGE OF MERCY

Sadly, we finish the story of Jonah with him angry at God for forgiving the Assyrians. Again, I think we cannot sit in judgment of Jonah. Israel killed the prophets who God sent pleading with them to repent. When Jonah went to a pagan nation, they spontaneously began fasting. Going back to our hypothetical world, that would be like Americans starting to kill Christian leaders for their message and the leaders and rank and file of Al-Qaeda repenting and turning to the Lord.

But for our purposes, we can focus on the good that came out of this story. In particular, we can focus on God's final words to Jonah:

> But Nineveh has more than a hundred and twenty thousand people who cannot tell their right hand from their left, and many cattle as well. Should I not be concerned about that great city?"

> Jonah 4:11

God was concerned for a city of 120,000 people. America has over 300 million. Is God concerned with us?

Of course He is.

One thing that is interesting is that what Jonah was told to tell the Ninevites is never revealed. We are never told what the sins of the Assyrians were that God was going to judge them for.

The message we are to understand from Nineveh is that no matter what our sins are, God is more than willing to forgive us and turn away from destroying us. Like the father in Jesus' parable of the prodigal son, our Father is watching for us to return from afar. He is waiting with an eager heart for us to listen to Him.

The story of Jonah is that it does not matter who we are, what we have done or how far we have gone, God will have mercy on us if we cry out in time. Nineveh had forty days to repent before God destroyed them and they did not test Him in His mercy. They chose to repent in three days.

HOW CAN WE RESPOND?

The message from the book of Jonah is one of the most pertinent to us today in America. Will repentance solve all our problems? No. A heart-felt move toward God is not going to make all our challenges immediately go away. In fact, in a nation as large as ours, there will always be challenges. There will always be struggles. What we have before us is not a call from God to turn to Him to fix our problems but an offer from God to persist as a nation.

Our options that face us are: 1) we repent and continue as a sovereign nation full of all the problems, challenges and freedom to govern ourselves, or 2) God sends judgment upon us and we lose our sovereignty. We no longer have the ability to wrestle with the challenges and political divides because we no longer control our own destiny.

If option 2 sounds far-fetched, you have not studied history. Every nation in history that has suddenly lost their sovereignty I am sure felt the same way. The number of haughty Titanics throughout history is truly staggering. How many unsinkable ships throughout the generations have been sunk before seemingly unworthy icebergs? How often have great military, cultural and financial stalwarts been reduced to nothing in short order?

Do not think it cannot happen because if we as God's people choose not to repent then it can, and most certainly will, happen. God does not send His messages of judgment because He longs to destroy, but because He longs to see people made right. He longs for justice, mercy and righteousness. However, unlike an undisciplined father that makes threat after threat against his children that he has no intention of keeping, God will certainly keep His word.

If Nineveh had not turned after forty days, they most certainly would have been destroyed. If we do not repent before our time is up, we will most certainly experience the judgment of God.

The good news is that God is willing to forgive us. He is willing to relent from judgment if we repent.

Let's not wait forty days. Let's choose to use today.

Chapter 10
ISRAEL AND JUDAH
A Case Study of Judgment

What happens when God does judge a nation? I pray we will not find out, but I am saddened by the response I have seen so far from the church in America. We seem to be growing more like the people of Judah leading up to their eventual judgment and destruction by Babylon than we do the people of Nineveh.

For several generations God sent prophet after prophet to plead with Judah to repent of their wickedness. Every single one of them was martyred for their message. Jeremiah was the last of the prophets God sent to plead with Judah to return to Him, and he would have been killed for his message too if the king had not been so intimidated by him.

The false prophets of Judah for generations proclaimed peace and safety. "God cannot judge us because He loves us; we are His people," or so their message went. The people of Judah engaged in all manner of wickedness while their false prophets proclaimed God's great love and tolerance for them.

Are we so different today? It seems the more wicked our nation grows the more voices we have within the church that are willing to stand up and proclaim God's great love over "His nation." The arrogance and indifference to God's Word that we show is only paralleled by the story of Judah before their destruction. But there is still hope.

ASKING THE RIGHT QUESTIONS

We can learn about our current situation from what happened to Judah and Israel. We have a much better record of God's Word to Judah before their destruction and captivity, but we also need to learn from Israel (the northern kingdom of Hebrews) and their outcome as well.

We must start by asking the right questions. Often in church people learn to read scripture and see how bad the Israelites were without any concern for what we are supposed to learn from them. Many people today are blind to how similar we truly are. The same sentiment we have now existed in Jesus' day when the leaders of Israel proclaimed, "If we had lived in the days of our forefathers, we would not have taken part with them in shedding the blood of the prophets" (Matthew 23:30).

They did not realize the tragic irony in that statement since they were soon to shed the blood of the greatest prophet of all. How could they be so blind?

They had studied scripture and were sure they had learned the right lessons from it. They had learned what made their forefathers so wrong. They had learned how not to be that way. But those were the wrong lessons. They were asking the wrong questions.

Instead of learning what they did and why their forefathers went so wrong, the Pharisees and leaders of Israel should have asked, "How did our forefathers miss it so badly? Why did they not see what we can see so clearly with hindsight?" In the end, the leaders in Jesus' day did not put themselves into the story to understand how they could possibly be just as bad as the leaders who had gone before them. They just assumed that since they knew the stories they would not repeat history.

Instead of saying, "I know what they did and I will not do it now," they should have been asking, "In what ways am I exactly like them? In what ways am I vulnerable to make the very same mistakes they did." It is often said that "those who do not know history are doomed to repeat it." In truth, the phrase should be, "Those who do not learn the appropriate lessons from history are doomed to repeat it." Often those lessons are lost on us because we refuse to acknowledge that we are of the same nature as those who went before us.

"We are much more civilized today." Ever heard that phrase? I have heard it as self-righteous justification many times as to why we would never have another World War II. The thinking goes that we would not allow such a heinous mindset to persist in our world today, and we certainly would not become Nazi Germany ourselves.

Men's ambitions, greed and evil desires have caused them to start wars and commit unspeakable atrocities in generations past, but for some reason we are different now. I do not know what changed, but the sad fact is that our arrogance in thinking that we are different is also nothing new.

If we do not ask ourselves how we are blind to the same problems as those who went before us, we will certainly repeat their sins. Unfortunately, God's people are doing just that right now.

ISRAEL

Israel's story is a sad one. From the moment they separated from Judah they rebelled against God. Jeroboam was given the kingdom of Israel directly by God (1 Kings 11:26-40) and almost immediately turned away from Him. Jeroboam was afraid that if Israel's religion stayed identical to Judah's (which required them all to make a pilgrimage to Jerusalem), he would lose his kingdom. His answer? He made new gods for Israel (1 Kings 12:25-33).

Jeroboam introduced a sinful lifestyle into Israel from day one that they never overcame. Prophets came and prophets went and very few listened. Jezebel, Israel's King Ahab's wife, killed thousands of prophets of God in order to silence them. She wanted the people to worship her gods (I Kings 16-22).

Israel was at almost constant war with Judah and almost always enjoyed the upper hand until their ultimate demise. They were told over and again to repent or the Lord Himself would judge them. God fulfilled His promise by sending Assyria to destroy and carry Israel away captive.

> 22 The Israelites persisted in all the sins of Jeroboam and did not turn away from them 23 until the Lord removed them from his presence, as he had warned through all his servants the prophets. So the people of Israel were taken from their homeland into exile in Assyria, and they are still there.
>
> 2 Kings 17:22-23

TRAGIC IGNORANCE

2 Kings 17 lists many of Israel's sins. Chief among them is that they turned away from the Lord, but the manner in which they did it is especially heinous. It says they followed the practices of the pagan nations who went before them.

Israel knew why God had given them the land while destroying the nations before them. Idol worship, corruption, murder and sexual immorality were the undoing of the nations God destroyed before Israel and Judah. God sent Israel prophets to remind them of this, but they chose not to listen.

That is what makes Israel's ignorance tragic. It was not that they were truly ignorant but that they chose ignorance for themselves. They chose not to listen. They chose not to study or believe their own history. Are we so different today?

While many of the stories of how America displaced the natives who lived here first are tragic, is it such a different story from Israel's that God allowed a nation espousing His views to displace a land of pagans? If through blood, sweat and tears the Lord gave this land to us who live here today, do we not owe God the same reverence He demanded from Israel, if not more?

GOD'S LOVED ONES

Israel was God's chosen people. America is not. America's foundation may be providential, but we must not think more of ourselves than we ought to. If God did not spare Israel judgment and exile, why would He spare us?

> 17 If some of the branches have been broken off, and you, though a wild olive shoot, have

been grafted in among the others and now share in the nourishing sap from the olive root, 18 do not consider yourself to be superior to those other branches. If you do, consider this: You do not support the root, but the root supports you. 19 You will say then, "Branches were broken off so that I could be grafted in." 20 Granted. But they were broken off because of unbelief, and you stand by faith. Do not be arrogant, but tremble. 21 For if God did not spare the natural branches, he will not spare you either. 22 Consider therefore the kindness and sternness of God: sternness to those who fell, but kindness to you, provided that you continue in his kindness. Otherwise, you also will be cut off.

Romans 11:17-22

America is a "wild olive branch" nation. If God would not spare His own chosen nation, He will not spare us. We must not confuse God's grace for pacifism in the face of sin and rebellion.

Our secret sins, just as Israel's (2 Kings 17:9), are coming to light in the form of our open rebellion against God. We are in the midst of redefining what is right and wrong so that we can assure ourselves that God could not possibly cut off a nation that He loves.

God certainly loves us, but in our present state that should cause us to be in fear, not confidence. If God loves us, He will not overlook our sins. He will not withhold His hand from our course. He will not for us because He did not for Israel and he did not for Judah.

JUDAH

We have more information in scripture about Judah's days leading up to judgment and destruction. Isaiah and Jeremiah both have a wealth of information to share about Judah's sins, their coming judgment and the continual rejection of their message.

Judah's "day of no return" came during the reign of King Manasseh. 1 Kings 21 says he "filled Jerusalem form end to end" with innocent blood, set up pagan altars in the temple and caused his people to completely turn away from their God.

God pronounced His judgment against Judah at that point, which we know He carried out with no concern for "His people." God did not restrain His hand from destroying His own temple, His own people, and His own city which Revelation tells us He will dwell in forever.

But unlike Israel, something different happened to Judah. We have much to learn from the story of Judah because in it lies a great hope America currently has.

THE POWER OF REPENTANCE

Manasseh, the most evil king Judah ever had, put the final nail in the coffin of Judah. God pronounced His sure judgment against His people because of Judah's sin during his reign. But the story in 2 Kings 21 is not the whole story.

2 Chronicles sheds a little more light on the situation that is critical for us to understand. The books of Kings and Chronicles are concurrent histories told with different points and different messages. They do not contradict each other, but sometimes stories in one are left out of another for one reason or another.

In 2 Chronicles 33 we find out that after God pronounced judgment against Manasseh, He swiftly carried it out. God had Assyria attack Jerusalem and take captive Manasseh and many people. Jerusalem was not completely destroyed; the Assyrians did not kill Manasseh. They bound him and threw him in jail in Babylon.

From Babylon, Manasseh cried out to the God his father, Hezekiah had known. He repented and asked for God's forgiveness, and God heard Him. Not only did God hear him, but God restored Manasseh as king of Judah (2 Chronicles 33:13)!

Manasseh was the most wicked king of Judah, presiding over the most rebellious people of Judah who all caused God to pronounce His judgment against them. Even after all this, God forgave Manasseh when he repented. God did not forget His decree of judgment against Judah; it was still coming, but He still had mercy on Jerusalem.

God put off the eventual destruction of Jerusalem for several generations because of Manasseh's repentance. God had already chosen to destroy Israel for their sin and rebellion, but because He found men willing to humble themselves before Him, He stayed His hand for a while.

WHO KNOWS?

This brings us back to the strange statement in Joel 2:14; "who knows?" At this point God had already pronounced His judgment against Judah and He had even carried it out to a very small degree. But men chose to repent. Manasseh led them in repentance by breaking down all the pagan altars he had set up. The nation joined in with him.

Even after Judah's sentence from God, He relented even if it was only for a time. We have already seen that Jonah knew this about God all too well. He knew that God is so ready to relent from judgment and destruction that if just a few people will repent God will spare a nation on their behalf. It was ten for Sodom. It was one for Judah, if even for a reprieve of forty years.

God is truly gracious and compassionate, but He is not blind. He is not deaf. He will act on behalf of the oppressed, murdered and abused. But He is waiting.

Longing. Listening. Will He hear us cry out to Him and humble ourselves?

JUDAH REVERTS TO SIN

After Manasseh died, his ancestors reigned in Judah. Josiah, his grandson, was the greatest and most righteous king of Judah since David. He restored much of the knowledge of God that was lost through the reigns of Judah's sinful rulers, but God's judgment still loomed. Once he died, Judah quickly began to experience God's judgment.

It is impossible to know whether God would have relented further from destroying Judah if the people had continued in Josiah's ways, but we know they did not. Josiah's son Jehoahaz was quickly destroyed by Egypt and his brother, Eliakim took his place. He soon suffered the same fate at the hand of Babylon.

A little over twenty-two years after Josiah's death, Jerusalem was completely destroyed and its inhabitants carried off to Babylon. God's judgment was sure. Judah had passed the point of no return during Manasseh's days; now they had run out of time. No more kings repented. The people would not listen to God's prophets any more. Time was up.

LESSONS FROM EXILE

Destruction and exile were not the end of Judah's story. The Bible would end with 2 Kings if it had been. No, we have much to learn from Judah even after their judgment.

Jeremiah prophesied to the people before their judgment that it was too late now. God had pronounced judgment in the days of Manasseh, and during the days of Jeremiah He pronounced His timing. The end had come, but the people refused to recognize it.

It is interesting to note that even though God was going to judge Judah, He still had a plan for them. In fact, none of His plans had been derailed. None of His promises had been voided. They were all still there, and we reap the benefits of them today.

God had a plan to protect and preserve Judah even during a time of tragic death, destruction and captivity. Jeremiah told the people that if they would accept it, God would deal gently with them. If they chose to continue to fight, He would increase their burden.

God's judgment was not about His hatred. It was not about His anger.

It was about His love.

ALWAYS HOPE

God was using the least amount of pain to produce the greatest amount of righteousness He could in Judah. The more they turned away, the greater the heat God turned up.

Judah's transition to the exile was bloody and devastating, but His provision for them in Babylon and Persia was astounding. The books of Daniel, Ezekiel, Ezra, Nehemiah and Esther all tell the stories of God's continuing provision, protection and supernatural power for those who were called by His name.

Judah's destruction was complete, but it was not final. God restored them to their land and rebuilt the ruins. And consider this: for over 1,000 years Israel had struggled with idolatry. No king, not even David, had been able to completely rid Israel of idols and the worship of foreign gods. After the Babylonian captivity, there is no record of the Jews ever turning to other gods again.

No matter what, we always have hope. Even though we have forsaken God, He will never forsake us. There is always hope that we can turn back to God and receive a blessing. There is always hope that God will heal our land.

Judah teaches us that God will not turn away from judgment, even against the ones He loves the most, but that there is always hope for a brighter future.

Before, during and even after judgment.

Chapter 11
THE LORD'S FAVOR
How Then Shall We Live?

Jesus walked into a synagogue in Nazareth one day and read from the prophet Isaiah. What He said and what followed is important for us to understand today.

> 18 "The Spirit of the Lord is upon Me,
> Because He has anointed Me
> To preach the gospel to the poor;
> He has sent Me to heal the brokenhearted,
> To proclaim liberty to the captives
> And recovery of sight to the blind,
> To set at liberty those who are oppressed;
>
> 19 To proclaim the acceptable year of the Lord." 20 Then He closed the book, and gave it back to the attendant and sat down. And the eyes of all who were in the synagogue were fixed on Him. 21 And He began to say to them, "Today this Scripture is fulfilled in your hearing." 22 So all bore witness to Him, and marveled at the gracious words which

proceeded out of His mouth. And they said, "Is this not Joseph's son?"

23 He said to them, "You will surely say this proverb to Me, 'Physician, heal yourself! Whatever we have heard done in Capernaum, do also here in Your country.' " 24 Then He said, "Assuredly, I say to you, no prophet is accepted in his own country. 25 But I tell you truly, many widows were in Israel in the days of Elijah, when the heaven was shut up three years and six months, and there was a great famine throughout all the land; 26 but to none of them was Elijah sent except to Zarephath, in the region of Sidon, to a woman who was a widow. 27 And many lepers were in Israel in the time of Elisha the prophet, and none of them was cleansed except Naaman the Syrian."

28 So all those in the synagogue, when they heard these things, were filled with wrath, 29 and rose up and thrust Him out of the city; and they led Him to the brow of the hill on which their city was built, that they might throw Him down over the cliff. 30 Then passing through the midst of them, He went His way.

Luke 4:18-30

ELIJAH'S DAY

It seems strange that what started out as such a good message ended so badly. Jesus was proclaiming to these people the greatest message they had ever heard. He was telling them the day they had been waiting for was here after many generations. The promises of the Lord were being fulfilled before their eyes.

But Jesus did not stop there. He knew the hearts of those listening. He knew their cold rebellion to the things of the Lord. He knew their desire to be honored, esteemed and praised. He knew the wickedness that lay beneath the surface of their countenance. They were able to hide it from others, but not from Jesus.

Jesus told them, in essence, that even though it was the year of the Lord's favor for many, it was not for them. Later, Jesus would speak even more plainly to these religious leaders and tell them that the judgment for them would be even more severe than for Sodom and Gomorrah on the day they met God face to face. In the same message where Jesus proclaimed some of the best news He ever spoke, He also pronounced a piercing judgment against those hearing.

God sent Elijah to a Gentile with a message of comfort and hope in one of the darkest days of Israel's history. Why? Because not one of God's chosen people would accept the message He had sent.

This made those in that synagogue so angry they immediately purposed to kill Jesus. We know that it was not His time, so He had no trouble putting a stop to their plot, but the anger this stirred up is troubling.

I see the same kind of anger today when the topic of judgment is brought up in context to the church. Why is it so hard for God's people to accept that if we stray from His will that our Good Shepherd will come and bring us back with the painful blows of His staff? His correction may hurt, but His desire is to have us always in the safety and provision of His presence.

WHERE HAVE WE STRAYED?

The church in America, in rejecting God's judgment over us, has strayed far away from God. We have been teaching the same thing the false prophets taught in the days before Israel and Judah's judgment--that God loves us too much to judge us.

Nothing could be further from the truth or more dangerous for us to think. God is the judge of everyone; we will all stand judgment face to face at an appointed time. The American flag will not stand before God someday; that is reserved for individuals alone. Until then, God judges nations and peoples in this temporal age.

If a people become so corrupt or a nation becomes so oppressive that people cry out to God, He will act on their behalf. He always has and He always will. As

God's people we must acknowledge that is His right and that He is always good when He does it.

America has become horribly corrupt. The poor are constantly oppressed for the benefit of the rich. Bribes flow freely. Justice is perverted on a regular basis. Sin has been called good and good has been called sin. We murder, lie, cheat and steal on biblical proportions.

Our nation has so radically turned away from God it would be unthinkable to me for any believer to defend our direction. What is truly sad about our situation is that the church has done just that. The church has been completely complicit and at times even involved in the sin and corruption our nation espouses.

In my dream about the rebuilt World Trade Center building, God made it very clear that it was Christians rebuilding the tower. Everyone was very happy, and it seemed very patriotic, but there was one big problem: the one in charge of the project was Satan.

Christians in America have unwittingly chosen the wrong side simply because we have not asked the right questions, if any at all. Christians in the US have overwhelmingly supported war, search and seizures, defiance to God's warning and judgments, and almost every other wayward action of our nation.

Instead of asking God what He was saying and thinking after 9/11, the church collectively set its hands to rebuilding what God was trying to destroy.

God wants those institutions that oppress gone. He wants those systems that pervert justice eradicated.

It is not that every system and every administration in our nation is evil, it is just that we never asked. God was seeking contrition and repentance. What we gave Him was defiance.

One very clear sign of this is the anger that so many people display when this topic is breached. The church reacts especially violently to the notion that God would judge America. That is not good; not good at all.

It is okay to take issue and wrestle with the idea that God would judge America. There are always doomsday naysayers out there and we should rightly have a healthy amount of skepticism, but to reject outright the notion that God could or would judge America is biblically unconscionable.

So far America has not responded well to God's gentle correction. Stock market crashes, unemployment and unthinkably high government reliance rates may not seem gentle, but a quick survey of history will inform us that God is more than willing to get our attention with much worse.

Our question is, will we choose to change before it is too late? Will we personally repent and call for repentance while there is still time?

WHAT DO WE DO?

We cannot make individual judgments like Jesus did against those who heard Him at the synagogue in Nazareth that day because we do not have access to the same information He had. We cannot see the heart; only God can do that. We can, however, see and hear clearly what God is saying to a people who call His name but have wandered far away from Him.

We cannot go "demon-hunting," searching for and calling out each person we believe to be outside God's will. That is not our place and it can actually be more destructive than the problems we currently have. Our task is to plead with God's people to look inside their own hearts and ask their loving Father to judge them. And we have to lead the way by looking inside our own hearts first.

David said it best when he said,

> Create in me a pure heart, O God, and renew a steadfast spirit within me.
>
> Psalm 51:10

and also when he said,

> Search me, O God, and know my heart; Try me, and know my anxieties; And see if there is any wicked way in me, And lead me in the way everlasting.
>
> Psalm 139:23-24

David was asking God to judge him. David knew he was dealing with a righteous judge, and he trusted God to deal fairly with him. David knew that God went even further than dealing fairly with him; he knew God would be more gracious with him than he deserved.

Many times in David's life he sinned in ways deserving death (2 Samuel 6, 11, 24) but God spared his life. Why? Was David more deserving than others who received God's harsh punishment? No, David was in some cases more deserving of death than others. So why did God have mercy on him?

REPENTANCE.

David, when faced with his sin, was always quick to acknowledge it and seek God's face for forgiveness. David was a perfect example of our relationship to God. None of us is deserving of the precious life that God grants to us every new day. We have all sinned and gone astray, and we are all under the eternal judgment of God.

But if we accept God's son, Jesus, we have the hope of life, and life eternally. When we understand our relationship to God as David did, it puts things in proper perspective. We do not overcome this life by not sinning. If God judges our nation, it will not be because we have begun sinning more than we did before.

No, God will judge us because we have stopped repenting of sin. He will judge us because we refuse to acknowledge our creator's great grace over each and every breath. God is patient with sin because He sees our frailty. He knows our flesh is weak (Matthew 26:41) and He bears long with us (Luke 18:7).

The apostle John had this to say:

> If we claim to be without sin, we deceive
> ourselves and the truth is not in us.
>
> 1 John 1:8

This is a scary statement. By refusing to acknowledge our sin, we tell the world that God's truth and love is not in us. Should we think that our Good Shepherd would let us slip so far so that this is true of us? No!

God disciplines those He loves (Proverbs 3:12, Acts 17:11, Hebrews 12:6) so that such a statement can never be true of His people. We never enjoy His discipline at the time, but it is always for our good.

WHERE WILL WE GO FROM HERE?

The Lord shared a clear message with me. He got my attention with the first dream about the World Trade Center, and I understood the message of the second dream. God is seeking repentance from a wayward nation. Without it He will surely bring judgment.

God has chosen to use a building that symbolizes our great defiance and resistance to those things that would choose to crush us. God was seeking repentance in the days of 9/11, but His people chose to make it off-limits to suggest those acts were possibly judgment from God trying to wake us up.

The little worship movement that ended quickly that I saw in the dream did happen. A few repented for a short time, but the nation ended up leaving the doors open to demons that came back with their friends who were even more evil (Luke 11:26).

The message of the Lord to me was that when the construction of 1 World Trade was done that it would be "a sign and seal of the judgment against America." He tied that sign and seal to the issue of homosexuality in my dream, not to say that we will be judged for homosexuality but to show a concurrent sign from scripture. As I have said before, Paul clearly told us in Romans 1 that societal acceptance of homosexuality is a sign that God has given people totally over to their evil desires for which they will receive judgment.

So where do we go from here? I believe we have three possible avenues we can take that coincide with the three case studies I have explained:

1. **Nineveh**: Repent before the completion of 1 World Trade Center and receive God's blessing on our land.

2. **Judah**: Repent after the completion of 1 World Trade Center and hope for the "who knows?" of the Lord that Joel promised.

3. **Sodom and Gomorrah**: Choose not to repent and be destroyed. We will lose our sovereignty and cease existence as a nation.

NINEVEH

God longs for "His people, who are called by His name" to repent and lead the way in this nation. I believe He has given us a time frame after which we have no going back. I do not know the date and hour, but I know it is tied to the completion of One World Trade Center. I do not want to wait another day.

I do not know how many God will require to repent before He grants us a pardon from judgment, but I am sure if enough do repent He will. Join me in calling as many people to repentance as you can and pray with me that God will accept the number. Lead the way in repentance. Ask God how you have been complicit with the sins of our nation and turn to Him with all your heart.

Choose to fast for your sins and the sins of our nation. I encourage you to set aside a day a week to fast for repentance in America.

Gather your church together for "solemn assemblies" like the one Joel calls for in Joel 2.

We cannot respond too "fanatically" to the call for repentance. God will honor our desire to return to Him. And remember, the only way we can respond is at the foot of the cross. We have no righteousness of our own.

JUDAH

I truly believe that if we do not repent until after the completion of One World Trade Center, then America's sovereignty will be shaken. That may sound extreme, but history does not lie. I believe that if the day comes and goes that the Lord has set then we can only hope to lessen or shorten our days of judgment. Maybe the Lord will grant us a reprieve.

If the day comes and goes and we have not repented, it is not time to give up hope. The story of Judah tells us that God will always hear the cry of repentance. We still have hope, even if our hope is in the days of the most trouble our nation has ever faced.

Remember the stories of Daniel, Shadrach, Meshach and Abednego. Remember Esther, Mordecai and Ezekiel. Remember Nehemiah and Ezra. Remember what came from the Jews even after the Babylonian captivity: Jesus, our redeemer.

Even if America's sovereignty is challenged (understand that I mean temporarily lost, if even in part), our best days may yet be ahead of us. A pronouncement of judgment from God is not the time for His people to give up, but to shine even brighter.

God will sustain us, protect us and supernaturally provide for us if we fall on our faces and seek Him in humility.

SODOM AND GOMORRAH (AND ISRAEL)

If after the day of judgment comes and goes and we choose not to repent, I fear that God will take away our place among the nations. I feel we will be more like Israel (displaced and lost as a people) than Sodom and Gomorrah (completely destroyed), but neither are good options.

I pray that we will not go this way. I have faith that America will respond to God after judgment and I have hope that we will repent before God's decree of judgment.

PRAYER IS THE SOLUTION

There is an entire book of the Bible named "Judges." The storyline of Judges repeats itself over and over. God's people, Israel, would turn away from Him and He would then remove His hand of protection from them. The surrounding nations would oppress Israel until they cried out to God for help.

That cry is what God is waiting for. What Israel was doing when they cried out was asking God to rescue them from their trouble, but it always came in a spirit of repentance. When Israel cried out to God for help, He would release a new champion to rescue Israel. They called these champions the judges.

During this period of the judges Israel could not choose for themselves a judge who would rescue them from their oppressors; they always failed. The judge who would save Israel always came from the Lord when they cried out for help, acknowledging again that they needed God alone to rescue them.

Many people today believe if we raise up awareness of the problems we face, we could collectively solve them. Education and a spirit of cooperation are key, as the thinking goes. This is true of political problems, as well as the problems the church faces today. Whereas education and cooperation are good things, they will not solve our problems now.

We have turned away from the Lord. No amount of education, awareness of issues or cooperation will rescue us. We must cry out. We must pray. Personally. Corporately.

If we try to focus on issues we feel will solve our problems and raise up champions for ourselves, we will most certainly fail. We must cry out to God in repentance and admit our need for He alone to rescue us. Only then will God raise up for us champions who will change the course of this nation.

We need champions in politics, finance, business, church and family, but only God can raise them up. He will only do that when He hears our cries.

When God hears our cries and raises up our modern-day judges, nothing can stand in their way. In the days of Israel's judges, when God appointed them, their enemies could not stand up to them. God's appointed judge, Gideon, defeated an entire army with only 300 men (Judges 6-8). God must be our primary leader. He must be our only hope. He alone must be our salvation.

Instead of first trying to fix your friends, community and nation, spend time in prayer and fasting. Our problems are too big for us to fix. That is the realization we must come to in order to fall on our knees in prayer.

If we cry out to God, He will answer us with hope.

WE NEED HOPE

It is hope that we need right now. Hope, if we act on it, becomes faith. If we commit ourselves to pray, fast and humble ourselves before God in repentance, then God will turn our hope into faith through bigger and bigger miracles in our nation.

Despair will not help and it will not turn away God's judgment. Only hope will. As a follower of Jesus, do not despair in the coming days. Even if we face increasing challenges and the pain of loss in the coming days, we are not a people who face tragedy and pain as those with no hope.

> 13 Brothers and sisters, we do not want you to be uninformed about those who sleep in death, so that you do not grieve like the rest of mankind, who have no hope.

> 1 Thessalonians 4:13

No matter what happens and no matter how bad things get, we will always have hope. We may grieve for the loss of our nation if it comes to that, but we have hope. Eternal hope.

In the end, America is not our home. We are visitors traveling through this land--strangers in a foreign land just like Abraham. Our citizenship is always in heaven first.

But as a patriot who loves his land, please join with me in humbling yourself through repentance. Cry out to God. Ask your friends and family to join you. Hold prayer meetings in your church to pray for your city, state and nation.

Join me as I hope and pray for our nation.

Because our time is short.

ABOUT THE AUTHOR

Darren Hibbs has worked in full-time ministry and the construction industry. As a writer, he has published several books.

Darren has great passion for revival in America and longs to see the church embrace God's correction so that we may receive the fullness of what He has to offer us.

Darren's heart burns to bring a message of hope to a lost and broken world through the immeasurable love of Jesus. It is his heart that this message of God's correction will be heard by the church and embraced so that the lost will see and hear the good news about Jesus as they see it change us.

Darren writes regularly and can be reached at www.JoelArmy.com.